the

DEEP THINGS

of GOD

JON PAULIEN

REVIEW AND HERALD® PUBLISHING ASSOCIATION
HAGERSTOWN, MD 21740

Other books by this author:
The Day That Changed the World
Knowing God in the Real World
Meet God Again—For the First Time
Millennium Bug
Present Truth in the Real World
What the Bible Says About the End-time

To order, call 1-800-765-6955.

Visit us at www.reviewandherald.com for information on other Review and Herald® products.

The author assumes full responsibility for the accuracy of all facts and quotations as cited in this book.

Unless otherwise noted, translations of Bible texts are the author's own.

Texts credited to NIV are from the *Holy Bible, New International Version*. Copyright © 1973, 1978, 1984, International Bible Society. Used by permission of Zondervan Bible Publishers.

This book was
Edited by Gerald Wheeler
Copyedited by James Cavil
Cover designed by Willie Duke/Leumas Design
Interior designed by Candy Harvey
Typeset: Bembo 11/14

PRINTED IN U.S.A.
08 07 06 05 04   5 4 3 2 1

R&H Cataloging Service
Paulien, Jonathan Karl, 1949-
    The deep things of God: an insider's guide to the book of Revelation.

    1. Bible. N.T. Revelation—Study and teaching.   2. Prophecy.
I. Title.

228

ISBN 0-8280-1812-X

CONTENTS

INTRODUCTION

You are vacationing on a lovely island. One day you walk along the edge of a cliff, occasionally stopping to peer over the edge at the waves crashing against the rocks below. The combination of wind, waves, and noise is exhilarating. Suddenly you stumble upon a very old man sitting on a flat spot near the top of the cliff with a great view of the coastline and the sea. His gaze fixed far out to sea, he doesn't seem to notice you.

"What are you looking at, sir?" you ask. "Are you waiting for a ship to come in?"

He doesn't answer.

Even when you approach closer, he still doesn't seem aware of your presence. Although his eyes are open, you get the impression that he is not really there with you, that his gaze is not focused on anything you can see.

"What are you looking at, sir?" you inquire again.

Again, no response.

Standing in front of him, you wave your hand before the man's eyes.

Still no reaction.

Torn between shaking the man, calling the police, and sitting down nearby to see what will happen next, you finally decide to take a seat and wait for a while to see what will happen.

After a few minutes the old man takes a deep breath, his eyes focus, and he glances around and sees you. You shift your posture a bit in case you need to get up and run in a hurry, but he smiles in a friendly way and says, "I suppose you are wondering what is going on."

Cautiously you nod.

Smiling again, he begins, "You probably won't believe this, but I just had an encounter with Jesus Himself! And He told me all about the future and what the end of the world will be like. I can't wait to share the message with someone. Would you be interested in hearing me out?"

Would you be interested? Or would you put him off as just another crank? When it comes to the book of Revelation, what thoughts fill your mind? The number 666? The Four Horsemen? The battle of

Armageddon? The New Jerusalem? The book of Revelation has intrigued people for nearly 2,000 years. It is an ambiguous, strange, and challenging book. And if you have been studying Revelation for any time at all, you have noticed that people have strong opinions about it. You also know that those opinions usually don't agree. Someone has suggested that if you find 12 Christians interested in the book of Revelation they will probably hold at least 13 different views on the book.

Since the book of Revelation claims to tell about the future, however, it still attracts our attention no matter how difficult it may be to understand. To be curious about the future seems to be a basic human drive. We all would like to know what is about to happen in our personal lives, our country, and the world. The problem is that when we open the book of Revelation the power of our curiosity can cause us to see what we want to see, rather than what is really there. Our passion to know can cloud or sway our knowing.

Those who misread Revelation today are far from the first to do so. But history tells us that misinterpreting Revelation is not ethically neutral. In the wrong hands the Apocalypse can be as dangerous as a terrorist attack. Sober and careful study of the Apocalypse is not just a game—it can be a life-and-death matter. For example, in A.D. 1534 a group of people studied the book of Revelation and concluded that the city of Münster, Germany, was the New Jerusalem. Many people perished in the battles fought over the city. Others starved to death in the siege that followed. Mistaken ideas about Revelation can be deadly. And not just in the distant past.

In 1993 the Branch Davidian standoff in Waco, Texas, seized the attention of a nation. The Davidians at Mount Carmel had sincerely and honestly studied the book of Revelation. But in the process they developed ideas that caused them to challenge the federal government of the United States in battle, ending up in the loss of nearly 100 lives. Men, women, and even little children found themselves sacrificed on the altar of someone's unique interpretation of the book of Revelation.

Perhaps the wiser course, then, would be to stay away from this book! After all, why go looking for trouble? But I don't think that's the answer either. Revelation is far too influential in today's world to ignore. The language of Revelation, from Armageddon to 666, has spread widely through popular culture. The kinds of themes addressed in the book are the subject of such influential and popular movies as *The Terminator, The Lion King, The Matrix,* and *Independence Day.* So whether we like it or not, understanding the book of Revelation is important in today's world. The best course, therefore, seems to involve learning *how to read* the book in a way that avoids the twin perils of fanaticism and indifference. Charting such a course is the purpose of this book.

Encouragement From Ellen White

An author that I've learned to appreciate, Ellen White, does not offer a detailed examination of the book of Revelation, but she saw special value in such study. A number of statements in her writings strongly encouraged me in my examination of this book. She comments, for example: "We do not understand the Word as we should. The book of Revelation opens with an injunction to us to understand the instruction that it contains. . . . We do not understand fully the lessons that it teaches, notwithstanding the injunction given us to search and study it."[1] Even though people have explored it for centuries, there is much more we need to learn about this book. The book of Revelation continues to require serious and careful attention.

Ellen White goes on to say that "when we as a people understand what this book means to us, there will be seen among us a great revival."[2] The book of Revelation has the potential to create a great Christian revival. "When the books of Daniel and Revelation are better understood, believers will have an entirely different religious experience."[3] What does that mean? "They will be given such glimpses of the open gates of Heaven that heart and mind will be impressed with the character that all must develop in order to realize the blessedness which is to be the reward of the pure in heart."[4]

The ultimate reason to study Revelation is that this strange book offers us a glimpse of heaven that you can't get anywhere else. You could say it presents heaven's secret intelligence about ultimate reality. Revelation takes us far beyond what we can see with a telescope. It opens up vistas that we cannot perceive with our eyes and ears. And when we understand the universe from God's perspective, we will have a much clearer picture of how to live successfully in that world that we *can* see, hear, and touch.

Let me share one last sentence from Ellen White: "The Lord will bless all who will seek humbly and meekly to understand that which is revealed in the Revelation."[5] According to this statement, attitude is everything. If my motivation for studying this book is to be able to show how brilliant I am, or to defend my pet ideas about the universe, I won't get the benefits that come only when I read with a spiritually hungry heart.

The farther you progress in your education, the more equipped you find yourself to solve problems and to master riddles. But truly educated people also realize how little they really know. They recognize the incredible variety of options in the process of learning. Although I have put several hours a day for the past 30 years into the study of this book, I have learned above all else that I have much more still to discover. A humble and meek approach to Revelation is the only sensible attitude to take.

Exploring the Basic Questions

When news reporters investigate a new best-seller, they examine the kind of person who wrote the book, when and where it was written, and how the author came up with the information presented. Such basic information is often crucial to understanding the book's goal and its message.

The Author of Revelation

From what the book itself tells us, the author of Revelation was a man named John (Rev. 1:9). He wrote to the Christian churches of Asia Minor, located in the western part of what we call Turkey today. Two thousand years ago these churches were part of the Roman province of Asia (verse 11). John seemed to have been some kind of authoritative figure among those congregations.

Several interesting features of the book of Revelation may shed some light on the kind of person he was. For one thing, the book contains numerous grammatical flaws in the original language (Greek). The Greek of Revelation reminds scholars of the practice writing of first-century schoolchildren (Greek samples of schoolwork exist among the papyrus documents unearthed in Egypt). So John was probably not a Greek speaker by either birth or training. Further evidence suggests that the author probably grew up in Palestine in a Jewish environment. If he had spent most of his life in Palestine and then moved to the Greek-speaking province of Asia, it would explain some of the difficulties he seems to have had with the Greek language. As a second language it was "Greek to him."

While the book of Revelation doesn't give us much detail about John, a number of other ancient documents address the issue. Most of them tell us that years before the book's composition John was one of the 12 disciples that walked with Jesus. He was the brother of James and the son of Zebedee. Jesus called him and his brother "sons of thunder" (apparently a reference to their loud and combative personalities—Jesus did have a sense of humor). According to such sources, John lived in Jerusalem for some 30 years, spent time in Pella across the Jordan, and then settled in Asia Minor some 50 years after the death and resurrection of Jesus. The tradition then tells us that during the final years of his life John wrote both the book of Revelation and the Fourth Gospel, the one that bears his name.

Many scholars question, however, whether the author of Revelation could be the same person as John, the disciple of Jesus and the author of the Gospel of John. The Gospel of John and the book of Revelation are quite different. While the grammar of the Gospel is simple, it is correct, and the book relates the life of Jesus in a stunning, masterful way. By way of contrast, the book of Revelation uses rough language to tell an apocalyptic story of strange beasts and perplexing symbols. Many scholars look at the stylistic differences and wonder how the same person could have written both books.

Other scholars, nevertheless, look at the two books and say, "Really, they do have lot in common." For one thing, both make much use of the number seven, if not directly, at least by implication. In the Gospel of John Jesus performs exactly seven miracles (no more and no less!) In the course of His ministry, and at many points in the book, we observe seven-day periods. The number seven is even more crucial to the book of Revelation, of course. Another common element in the two books is the use of the words "testimony" or "witness" to describe fidelity to the gospel, and how the imagery of "light" and "darkness" represent truth and error. Also, only the books of John and Revelation refer to Jesus as "the Word" of God (*logos* in the Greek).

Given the similarities between the two books, why are they so different? One possibility is that John, a Palestinian Jew living in Asia Minor, thought in Hebrew as he wrote in Greek. Stephen Thompson, an American scholar who has spent much of his career in England and Australia, demonstrates that the Greek in the book of Revelation is heavily influenced by Hebrew, or Semitic, thinking.[6] So John's Hebrew background may account for much, if not all, of the poor grammar in Revelation. But if that is the case, why is the Greek of the Gospel of John so beautiful?

I have a suggestion. As mentioned earlier, the author of the book of Revelation did not write from Ephesus or Smyrna or any of the other churches of Asia Minor, but from Patmos, an island some 40 miles off the coast of Asia Minor. No one knows for sure why John was on Patmos, but most external traditions tell us he was there as a prisoner. Perhaps Patmos was an ancient version of Alcatraz. If so, John was probably on his own when it came to composing the book. He wrote down the visions he received in his own words, grammatical flaws and all. If he had been at Ephesus, on the other hand, he could have had access to editorial help.

The evidence indicates that Paul had a lot of secretarial help, people who would take things he told them and write them up. So perhaps the difference between the Gospel of John and the book of Revelation is that John did not have access to editorial assistance when he was preparing the latter on Patmos. It would be fun to learn more about the person(s) who helped John shape his Gospel into the magnificent literary piece that it is, but information about that process is lost to history for now. With the evidence that is available to us, we will make the working assumption that the human author of Revelation is the same John that we learn so much about in the rest of the New Testament. The divine author of the book, of course, is Jesus.

The Date of Revelation

Did John prepare the book of Revelation early or late in his career? Do we have any idea as to a date of composition? Scholars generally hold two differing opinions on the subject. The minority view is that the book reflects the time of the emperor Nero, around A.D. 65. The majority view, supported by the bulk of the nonbiblical tradition, is that John wrote during the reign of Domitian, who reigned as emperor of Rome from A.D. 81 to A.D. 96. In the latter case the date is usually thought to be around A.D. 95, as some evidence suggests that John left Patmos shortly after finishing the book.

Scholars have considered both periods because of the indication that each of the two emperors persecuted Christians at some point. This ties in with the theme of martyrdom that appears throughout the book of Revelation. The first organized Roman persecution of Christians seems to have been the brief episode after the burning of Rome in the time of Nero. Some think that Nero himself set the fire and blamed the Christians in order to deflect attention from his own actions. On the other hand, Ireneaus, a Christian writer who flourished about A.D. 175-200, named Domitian as the emperor at the time of John's authorship of Revelation. Which of the two dates is more likely?

I prefer a late date for the book of Revelation, around A.D. 95 Before Domitian's time, Rome as an empire did not oppose Christians, at least not in any consistent fashion. In the book of Acts you will note that time and again Roman authorities rescued Paul from his enemies (Acts 18:12-17; 20:23-38; 21:27-22:29; 23:1-10; 23:12-35). So Rome was not hostile to Paul, or the Jews in general, during the time described in Acts. Nero's actions, while severe, seem more impulsive than systematic. They probably represent the isolated deeds of a mentally disturbed person.

The hostility of the Roman state toward Christianity in the second century A.D., on the other hand, resulted from the practice of emperor worship. One of the ways that the emperors of Rome kept people loyal was through a system of worship that actually regarded the emperor as a "god." In many parts of the empire people built temples in honor of the emperor, especially in the eastern territories. The emperors themselves did not seem all that interested in the idea at first (obviously they knew better). So we find little evidence for emperor worship during the first century, but when it does arise it seems to have originated in Asia Minor. The practice may have begun during the reign of Domitian, although the evidence is mixed. If John did compose Revelation at this time, its theme of martyrdom reflects a period of transition when systematic persecution of Christians was beginning and worse things were on the horizon.

How solid is the nonbiblical evidence tying the authorship of Revelation to the time of Domitian? Ireneaus, who wrote around A.D. 180, was a friend of Polycarp, who was martyred in A.D. 156. Polycarp was old enough at the time of his death that he would have been a young adult in A.D. 90-95 Irenaeus based his testimony regarding the authorship and date of Revelation on personal contact with Polycarp, who claimed to have known John personally. So while the external evidence is not conclusive, it points strongly in the direction of a late date for the book of Revelation—one toward the end of the first century.

"The Time Is Near"

I believe, however, that we have decisive biblical support for the idea that Revelation was written late in the first century. We find it when we compare certain texts in Revelation with Jesus' end-time sermon on the Mount of Olives, as recorded in Mark 13. Note Mark 13:28, 29: "Now learn this lesson from the fig tree: As soon as its twigs get tender and its leaves come out, you know that summer is near. Even so, when you see these things happening, you know that *it is near,* right at the door" (NIV).

In Mark 13 (a similar account appears in Matthew 24:32-35) Jesus was describing the future, telling the disciples what would occur between their time and His mighty and spectacular second coming. They had asked Jesus questions about the destruction of the Temple and the timing of His return (Matt. 24:3; Mark 13:4; Luke 21:5-7). The disciples didn't want Jesus to delay long, but longed for Him to come back as soon as possible. Recognizing their expectation, He explained that a series of "signs" would occur first: wars and rumors of wars, famines, earthquakes, heavenly phenomena, false prophets, and the gospel going to the world (Mark 13:5-23). Only when those events had taken place would His coming be "near, right at the door." What did Jesus have in mind here? That His return was not near at the time He was talking to His disciples. A number of things had to happen first. After all of them had taken place, *then* and only then would it be appropriate to say (in the words of Mark's account) *"It is near."*

Mark's account of Jesus' sermon continues in verse 33: "Be on guard! Be alert! You do not know when *that time* will come" (NIV). What time? The moment of Jesus' advent. You cannot know the time that Jesus will come, but you can know when it is near. Now notice the difference between the assertions of Mark 13:29-33 and the words of Revelation 22:10: "Then he told me, 'Do not seal up the words of the prophecy of this book, because *the time is near'"* (NIV).

Mark 13:29		"is near"
Mark 13:33	"the time"	
Rev. 22:10	"the time	is near"

As illustrated in English in the box on the previous page, Revelation 22:10 contains an exact verbal parallel to Mark 13 in the Greek. But in

Mark 13 Jesus said that "the time" would be imminent only after certain things had taken place. In other words, in A.D. 31 (when Jesus spoke) the time was not near. But by the date John had finished the book of Revelation, things had changed. The time was now near. What's the difference between the two statements? The contrast is the "all these things" of Mark 13:29. The "signs" that were to take place between when Jesus spoke and the time when His coming would be near had been fulfilled by the time John composed the book of Revelation.

To us today this whole issue makes little sense. We have seen nearly 2,000 years go by without the return of Jesus. Many of us are still looking for Jesus' signs of the end in today's world. How then could John and other Christians perceive that all those things had been fulfilled in the first century?

The key lies in the fact that Jesus blended two events in his end-time sermon of Mark 13—the destruction of the Temple (and Jerusalem) in A.D. 70 and the end of the world. While much of His end-time sermon applies particularly to the final generation of earth's history, by the time of the Temple's destruction Christian believers had plenty of evidence that the signs Jesus spoke about had already occurred. Let me share with you a little history of the first century.

Did false messiahs arise in the first century (Matt. 24:24; Mark 13:22)? In Acts 8:9-24 Simon the Sorcerer wanted to be a messiah figure, and Acts 5:36, 37 mentions a couple more "messiahs." The histories of Josephus, who wrote around A.D. 100, present even more examples of people who claimed to be a messiah during the first century, particularly in the era just before the destruction of Jerusalem in A.D. 70.

Did "wars and rumors of wars" circulate during the first century (Matt. 24:6, 7; Mark 13:7, 8; Luke 21:9, 10)? Very much so. While the *pax romana* (Roman peace) dominated the Empire at the time when Jesus spoke, that peace broke down widely in the sixties of that century, particularly in Palestine when the Jews revolted against Rome (A.D. 66-73). In the events of this "Jewish war" (so-called by Josephus) we see much of the fulfillment of the "all these things" that Jesus described.

What about Jesus' prediction about famine (Matt. 24:7; Mark 13:8; Luke 21:11)? History describes a terrible famine in Palestine around A.D. 46, one that Acts 11 appears to mention. Jesus also talks about pestilence or contagious disease (Luke 21:11). History tells us that in the time of Nero (A.D.

54-68) 30,000 people died of the bubonic plague (Black Death) in Rome in one autumn season.

Furthermore, Jesus predicted earthquakes (Matt. 24:8; Mark 13:8; Luke 21:11). In A.D. 60 one leveled the city of Laodicea. Another devastated Pompeii in A.D. 63 .And one even struck the city of Rome in A.D. 68. Earthquakes seem to have been a frequent occurrence in the Mediterranean area during the middle of the first century.

As for the signs in the heavens (Matt. 24:29, 30; Mark 13:24, 25; Luke 21:25), if you are familiar with the writings of Josephus, you are aware of his report that when the Roman armies surrounded the city of Jerusalem people saw tremendous apparitions in the sky, in addition to other remarkable events that they interpreted as signs.[7] Many regarded the phenomena as indicating that the Jewish cause was failing and the city of Jerusalem was doomed. If you don't have access to the writings of Josephus, you can find some of his descriptions in the book *The Great Controversy*.[8]

According to Jesus, His own disciples would experience persecution (Matt. 10:17-23; Mark 13:9-13; Luke 21:12-19). Were they also fulfilled in the first century? As mentioned earlier, the Roman Empire as a whole was fairly neutral toward Christianity during the first century, but the accounts in the book of Acts indicate that the early Christians suffered a great deal from those around them, particularly in their relationships with the synagogues and the Sanhedrin (Acts 4:1-22; 5:17-42; 6:8-15; 7:1-60; 8:1-3; 9:1, 2; 12:1-10; 13:45, 50; 14:5, 19, 20, etc.). Persecution was sporadic rather than systematic, yet it played a major role in first-century Christian experience.

False prophets would surface (Matt. 24:24; Mark 13:22). New Testament books such as 1 and 2 Corinthians, Galatians, Colossians, 2 and 3 John, and Jude contain abundant evidence that many people within the early church raised ideas that conflicted with those of Jesus and the apostles.

Perhaps the most prominent of Jesus' "signs of the end" was His assertion that the gospel would go to the whole world before His return (Matt. 24:14; Mark 13:10). While many have limited this prediction to the end of the world, the New Testament indicates that the apostles believed that it had in some way been fulfilled in their day. In Colossians Paul wrote: "This is the gospel that you heard and that has been proclaimed to every creature under heaven, and of which I, Paul, have become a servant" (Col. 1:23, NIV). Paul evidently had the impression that the gospel had already been preached to the world. It was "now revealed and made known through the prophetic writings by the command of the eternal God, so that all nations might believe and obey him" (Rom. 16:26, NIV; cf. 1:8).

And, finally, what about the great tribulation that Jesus talks about (Matt. 24:21, 22; Mark 13:19, 20)? Did it too have a fulfillment within the first century? Once again Josephus describes the horrific experience of the Jews in Jerusalem about 40 years after Jesus' sermon.[9] The suffering of the Jews around A.D. 70 was so powerful and so tragic as to set the tone for the sufferings of the end-time.

The preceding evidence shows how a first-century Christian could conclude that the signs of the end had been fulfilled within that first generation. If John was familiar with the end-time teachings of Jesus, and there is no question that he was, he seems to have believed that by the time he wrote Revelation he could describe the return of Jesus as imminent. And if he regarded the coming of Jesus as near, then he believed that the signs Jesus had said would precede His return, the "greening of the leaves before summer" (Matt. 24:32, 33; Mark 13:28, 29), had already taken place.

Here's the point of this whole exercise. If the author of Revelation can declare that "the time is near" (Rev. 1:3; 22:10), it is strong evidence that he did not compose the book of Revelation at the time of Nero. The signs we have described above were just beginning to be fulfilled in the 50s and early 60s of the first century. After the events surrounding the destruction of Jerusalem (A.D. 70) first century Christians could easily have decided that the signs of Jesus' return had met their fulfillment. This leads me to believe that the most likely of the two dates for the writing of Revelation is around A.D. 95, the very time recalled by second century Christian writers after the close of the New Testament canon.

How could John describe the Second Advent as near more than 1,900 years ago (Rev. 1:1, 3)? The return of Jesus was certainly not close in the chronological sense! It was, however, near in terms of God's desire to come and His desire for His people to be ready. Whether or not Jesus appears in our lifetime, the healthiest stance to take is that it is near for us. Not only that, a thorough study of Revelation indicates that the term "nearness" is especially appropriate to the times in which we live today. As we study this glorious and perplexing book, it will lead us to follow the instructions of Jesus in Luke 21:28: "When you see all these things taking place, lift up your heads, for your redemption draws near."

---

[1] Ellen G. White, *Testimonies to Ministers and Gospel Workers* (Mountain View, Calif.: Pacific Press Pub. Assn., 1923), p. 113.

[2] *Ibid.*

[3] *Ibid.*, p. 114.

[4] *Ibid.*

[5] *Ibid.*

[6] Steven Thompson, *The Apocalypse and Semitic Syntax,* Society for New Testament Studies Monograph Series, 52 (Cambridge: Cambridge University Press, 1985).

[7] Flavius Josephus *Wars of the Jews* 6, 5, 3, translated by William Whiston, in *Josephus: Complete Works* (Grand Rapids: Kregel Publications, 1960).

[8] Ellen G. White, *The Great Controversy* (Washington, D.C.: Review and Herald Pub. Assn., 1911), pp. 29, 30.

[9] Josephus *Wars of the Jews* 5, 6; cf. White, *The Great Controversy,* pp. 31-36.

1

THE WORLD OF THE BOOK OF REVELATION

I was born on the Upper East Side of Manhattan . . . when it was relatively poor (today the Upper East Side is the nation's most expensive real estate). My parents soon found affordable and attractive housing across the Hudson River in New Jersey. But while I now lived up in another state, my family and I still thought of ourselves as New Yorkers. We went to church in Manhattan, and when we could afford it, my brother and I went to Adventist schools in the city as well.

It was tough growing up Adventist in New York City. Not only were most of the people on the street secular, we didn't even feel at home with Christians of other denominations. We were a tiny community of our own in the midst of an enormous world of skyscrapers and forbidden attractions. Like most New Yorkers, we hurried from one familiar place to another through a vast jungle of strangers with unfamiliar faces. Each day we rode subways and buses crowded with people who labored diligently not to make eye contact or otherwise acknowledge each other's existence. To grow up Adventist in New York was to be a stranger in a strange land.

While I can't say that anyone ever really persecuted me for my faith, I knew that I was different, that I was strange. I wanted to be liked, but the neighbor kids knew that I was not one of them. I didn't go to the movie theaters with them and never showed up at the school dances on Friday night (I attended public school for five years). When my friends asked if they could come over on Saturdays I made some excuse or other. Offered a beer or a smoke I declined as politely as I knew how (although I suffered many guilty struggles at the neighborhood candy shop). When the pork chops came out at my friend's house, I made it clear that I was not hungry (even though I had been there for five hours). Persecuted? No. Abused? No. Scorned and rejected? Not really. My non-Adventist friends and neighbors were really nice people. A fish out of water? Yes. A stranger in a strange land? Definitely.

Growing up, I felt more at home in the book of Revelation than I did in my neighborhood. John seemed to understand my struggles with the world. Appreciating the lure of the forbidden attractions, the sense of being different and even weird, he set the table for the kind of world I was living in. When I studied about the seven churches, I felt as if I was reading about me. As a scholar of Revelation the more I learn about John's world the more it sounds like the one I grew up in. Christians in Asia Minor, even if they weren't persecuted, still struggled with how they should live in a pagan world.

Ancient Roman society met most human needs through one of two institutions: the family and the state. There was also a third category of society, what we might call "associations" or "clubs." Such associations existed to deal with needs not met by either the home or the government. In a way they were like an extended family. The church found its place in this ambiguous third category of society. Roman society regarded it as a strange sort of "club." Although Roman associations were generally harmless, at times the state felt threatened by them. According to Adela Yarbro Collins, five major events made the situation of the church in the Roman world seem increasingly precarious at the time John wrote Revelation.[1]

The Precarious Situation of the Church
Conflicts With the Jews

First of all, the church was suffering from a number of conflicts with the Jews that had potentially serious consequences. You see, the Romans considered Judaism a *religio licita,* the Latin term for a legal religion. As a legal religion Jews had privileges not granted to others, such as the right to Sabbath observance and to exemption from worship of the emperor. Rome had learned that cutting the Jews some slack avoided a lot of problems. As long as people regarded Christians as Jews, and many of them were, Roman law sheltered them.

Toward the end of the first century, however, disagreements between Christians and Jews threatened to separate them from each other in the minds of the general public. Since Jews were a recognized association and the church was not, the more the Roman Empire distinguished Christians from Judaism, the more difficulties the church would have in society. So Jewish attempts to repudiate Christianity had legal consequences for Christians in the first century. Note the evidence of the following texts:

"I know your afflictions and your poverty—yet you are rich! *I know the slander of those who say they are Jews and are not, but are a synagogue of Satan.* Do not be afraid of what you are about to suffer. I tell you, the devil will put some of you in prison to test you, and you will suffer persecution for ten days. Be faithful, even to the point of death, and I will give you the crown of life" (Rev. 2:9, 10, NIV).

"To the angel of the church in Philadelphia write: These are the words of him who is holy and true, who holds the key of David. What he opens, no one can shut; and what he shuts, no one can open. I know your deeds. See, I have placed before you an open door that no one can shut. I know that you have little strength, yet you have kept my word and have not denied my name. *I will make those who are of the synagogue of Satan, who claim to be Jews though they are not,* but are liars—I will make them come and fall down at your feet and acknowledge that I have loved you" (Rev. 3:7-9, NIV).

Some evidence suggests that Jews made note of the fact that Christians were the only Jewish sect that did not stay in Jerusalem and fight during the war of independence against Rome in A.D. 70. From that time on they increasingly viewed Christians as a foreign element, even when they attended the synagogues. A number of scholars believe that some Jewish leaders added an extra prayer or benediction to synagogue services around A.D. 80-90. This "eighteenth benediction" was basically a curse against Christ and Christians. Christians attending such a service would reveal themselves by falling silent during that benediction. When they did so the leaders could single them out and exclude them.

So around the time that John composed the book of Revelation the legal standing of Christians came under threat. They would naturally be concerned about this situation and wonder what the future would hold for them in Roman society.

Gentile Accusations

A second problem that Christians began to face at this time were ac-

cusations from their Gentile neighbors. As Gentiles came to see a distinction between Christian faith and Judaism, they often viewed Christianity
with hostile contempt. From the second century on we find plenty of evidence for Gentile accusations against Christians. It is reasonable to assume that such charges had already begun to occur toward the close of
the first century, although we have no direct written documentation.
Let's look at the kinds of allegations that Christians faced shortly after the
writing of Revelation.

One second-century accusation was that Christians were "haters of the
human race." The general public regarded them as exclusive because they
did not participate in civil society the way most people did. Pagan rituals
and rhetoric saturated public events in Asia Minor. Christians, therefore,
usually avoided them so as not to compromise their faith. The general pop-
ulation, on the other hand, took a smorgasbord approach to religion. They
felt free to pick and choose among a variety of ideas. But much like today,
they did not appreciate people who thought they had the truth and that everybody else was wrong. So they accused Christians of being anti-society.

Since religion was so tightly connected with civil affairs in ancient
Rome, Christians also endured complaints of "atheism" because they
would not worship any god but their own. The peoples of the Empire each
had their own religious preferences but added worship of the state gods as
a token of their allegiance to the state. Many charged Christians with atheism because they would not accept the state gods as objects of worship.

Christians, oddly enough, also got accused of "cannibalism." How on
earth did this one originate? It had to do with Gentile perceptions of the
Lord's Supper, in which Christians talked about "eating the body and
drinking the blood" of their Lord. Christians understood these statements
in a spiritual way, but apparently their pagan neighbors did not. So stories
went around that Christians sacrificed children and others in order to eat
at their Lord's table. The combined effect of all these accusations made it
an insecure world for Christians to live in.

Traumatic News

A number of traumatic events would have offered further indication
that Christian standing in Roman society was becoming increasingly uncertain. One such event was the destruction of Jerusalem. While it did not

affect Christians directly, it raised an important question: If the Romans could treat a *legal* religion in such a brutal manner, what would happen if the government focused its attention on Christians?

A second piece of traumatic news would have been reports of Nero's persecutions. While brief, they were gruesome. Though probably the work of an insane person, the helplessness of Rome's Christians showed just how fragile the relationship of all Christians to the Empire was. Roman society did not have a lot of safeguards for minorities. The modern Western world generally supports the idea that the legal system should prevent the majority from totally abusing a minority viewpoint. But in New Testament times it was not so. A Roman emperor could mistreat a minority with little danger of retribution.

A third piece of traumatic news was the gradual development of the imperial cult of emperor worship. The call to worship the emperor was both a religious and a political act. Refusal to participate in emperor worship was more than unpatriotic—it was treasonous, making it difficult for people to be good citizens and good Christians at the same time. The practice singled out Christians because even small tokens of loyalty to the emperor compromised their relationship with Jesus Christ. Asking Christians to worship the emperor would be like forcing Jews to become Nazis or African-Americans to give public lip service to the tenets of the Ku Klux Klan.

The Death of Antipas

The book of Revelation also reports the execution of a Christian named Antipas. While Scripture gives no details, it is clear that he died a martyr to his faith. "You did not renounce your faith in me, even in the days of Antipas, my faithful witness, who was put to death in your city— where Satan lives" (Rev. 2:13, NIV). Pergamum was one of the places where the Roman governor held court and made judicial decisions. It is possible that early Christians would see in the "sharp, two-edged sword" of Christ (verses 12, 16) a contrast to the governor's power over the "sword," the death sentence.[2] If so, the Roman governor probably executed Antipas for being a Christian.

The procedure in Antipas' case may have been that described by the governor Pliny some 15 years later in a letter he wrote to the emperor Trajan:

"I have asked the accused whether they were Christians. If they confessed, I asked a second and a third time, threatening penalty. Those who persisted I ordered to be executed, for I did not doubt that, whatever it was they professed, they deserved to be punished for their inflexible obstinacy. . . . I dismissed those who said they were not or never had been Christians, and who in my presence supplicated the gods and placed wine and incense before your [Trajan's] image, and especially cursed Christ, which I hear no true Christian will do."

Trajan responded that the local authorities should not seek out or try Christians on the basis of anonymous accusations, but if openly brought to the governor's attention, they were to be handled as Pliny had described.[3] The governor probably did not search out Antipas, but a hostile neighbor, either Jew or Gentile, accused him. Imagine living in a place where you never knew which neighbor might suddenly report your faith to the authorities! If it could happen to Antipas, it could happen to any Christian.

The Exile of John

Finally, of course, Christians would have been aware of John's own exile. Although recent scholarship has raised some questions about it, early church tradition widely held that the authorities had sent the beloved patriarch of the church in Asia Minor to the island of Patmos in order to prevent him from spreading his faith.[4] If the leader of the churches was now in exile, it would increase the sense of insecurity within the membership. The original readers of Revelation, therefore, seem to have been Christians whose position in society was becoming more and more precarious because of their faith. Concerned about where things were going in the future, they looked to John to provide direction and comfort in their situation.

Divisions in the Church

The Basic Situation

The situation of the churches in Asia Minor was even more precarious, however, for another reason. Christianity faced more than just threats from the outside. Divisions in the church itself endangered it from inside as well. The members of the congregations in Asia Minor vigorously disagreed about how to handle their marginalized position in society. We can see this very clearly as we work our way through the seven letters (Rev. 2; 3).

"Nevertheless, I have a few things against you: You have people there who hold to the teaching of Balaam, who taught Balak to entice the Israelites to sin by eating food sacrificed to idols and by committing sexual immorality" (Rev. 2:14, NIV). Apparently some Christians in Pergamos were following what Jesus calls the "teachings of Balaam." Balaam did not succeed in destroying the Israelites through prophetic curses. So instead he counseled the Moabites to use sexual enticement and idolatrous feasts (Num. 25:1-3; 31:16) to lead them away from God. The letters to the churches draw a strong tie between the temptations of Israel and the situation of the congregations in Asia Minor.

The majority of Christians in Pergamos, Ephesus, and Smyrna were faithful to God and to the course John had taught them. But a minority succumbed to the temptation to accommodate to the prevailing winds of their communities, and in the process John feared that they would lose their connection to Christ. But while these three churches were divided, the majority seem to have remained faithful. When you get to Thyatira, the fourth church, it begins to look more like a 50-50 split. Even some of the leaders of the church at Thyatira had taken positions on the wrong side.

The impression of degeneration continues in the last three churches. In Sardis, Philadelphia, and Laodicea the majority are not on John's side. "Yet you have a few people in Sardis who have not soiled their clothes. They will walk with me, dressed in white, for they are worthy" (Rev. 3:4, NIV). Especially in Sardis the faithful ones are few. While Philadelphia seems to have less problems with heresy, the church has little strength (verse 8). With Laodicea things are even worse. The letter gives the impression that the church is locking Jesus out (verse 20). The congregation doesn't even have a faithful minority. Jesus can find nothing good in Laodicea at all (verses 14-20).

So among the seven churches of Asia Minor three seem largely on John's side of the conflict, one seems to be about 50-50, and the last three have only a few who remain faithful. The churches of Asia Minor are seriously divided about how to relate to society and the problems around them. It is a period of both external and internal stress. So John wrote the book of Revelation not only to encourage the faithful in a time of impending persecution, but also to confront the churches about their fractured condition.

Beliefs of the Opposition

The seven letters of Revelation 2 and 3 offer a sharp rebuke to many in the churches. When we compare what we find in Revelation with other New Testament books, we gain some insight into the following questions: "Why were the Christians of Asia Minor divided? What was the basis for that division? Who were John's opponents, and what did they believe?"

Revelation 2 describes those who resist John by three different names: the Nicolaitans, Balaam, and Jezebel.

"Nevertheless, I have a few things against you: *You have people there who hold to the teaching of Balaam,* who taught Balak to entice the Israelites to sin by eating food sacrificed to idols and by committing sexual immorality. Likewise *you also have those who hold to the teaching of the Nicolaitans*" (Rev. 2:14, 15, NIV).

"Nevertheless, *I have this against you: You tolerate that woman Jezebel,* who calls herself a prophetess. By her teaching she misleads my servants into sexual immorality and the eating of food sacrificed to idols" (verse 20, NIV).

So the book calls John's opponents the followers of Balaam, Jezebel, and those who hold to the teaching of the Nicolaitans. Apparently all three names depict the same group, because all three names involve the same problems: the two basic issues of food offered to idols and sexual immorality. A further evidence of the unity between these groups emerges from the meaning of two of the names. "Nikolaos" is a Greek term that translates as "conqueror of the people," while the Hebrew term "Balaam" means "one who swallows up the people." Thus the two names represent essentially the same thing (one Greek and the other Hebrew).

So all three "groups" taught essentially the same thing—something to do with food offered to idols and sexual immorality. Interestingly enough, when you go to the writings of the following century the same two issues appear front row center. Why did such issues split Christians? Because they particularly involved how Christians related to the state and the society around them.

The Empire required all non-Jews to participate in Roman civil religion. The Romans tolerated all kinds of religious practices, but no matter what your religion was or where you came from, the government also expected you to take part in the ceremonies and public events of Roman society. Such events were somewhat like the Fourth of July parade in the

United States. It did not matter what religion you were; it was part of your duty as a citizen to join in.

Citizens who did not participate in the civil religion (the Jews, of course, were exempted) faced serious consequences, even apart from any death penalty. Those who did not take part in the civil ceremonies would lose significant economic opportunities. They would be ostracized from the trade guilds, in which people networked to build their businesses. When jobs opened up, the best would be reserved for the "good citizens" of the area. Noninvolvement also had political consequences. Civic positions required people to encourage and lead out in the civil religion. Without political position, Christians had no or little ability to influence the development of society or to improve their position within it. Lack of involvement in the civil religion also forfeited social opportunities. Just as today, the party crowd was also the "in crowd" and Christians had a hard time becoming "in." As a result, those who refused to participate in Roman civil religion became poor, powerless, and social outcasts. These were very real issues to anyone who considered becoming a Christian in first-century Asia Minor.

Why did Christians have so many problems with the Roman civil religion? Because two major elements in it would lead to a compromise with Christian faith: the issue of food offered to idols and the matter of "fornication." Why was food offered to idols a problem for John's churches? After all, in his first letter to the Corinthians, Paul says that an idol is nothing and offering food to an idol does not really matter because idols cannot speak, hear, or feel (1 Cor. 8:4, 7-9). Even if you offered something to an idol, nothing has really happened so in principle there is no big problem here. But by the time of Revelation, the situation seems to have changed. When Christians saw the idol feast as a way of putting the state before God, it would create a serious conflict for many of them.

The issue of cultic prostitution also caused problems. Ritualized prostitution formed part of the ancient religious scene. The idea seems to have been that if sexual intercourse took place in the temple rain would fall in abundance, the crops would grow, and the community would be prosperous. Society assumed that a good citizen would on occasion visit a temple prostitute simply to encourage a little rain at the proper time. As strange as this sounds to us, it made sense to the ancients. Some in the community might regard people who held aloof from such "civic traditions" as hostile to the community's welfare.

In the Western world today wealth and security seem to represent the highest goals of secular society. But the Greco-Roman world had an even more fundamental goal: status. It was a world that reveled in the honor and esteem of others and poured shame on those who did not conform. Thus the restrictions of Christian life and practice virtually guaranteed exclusion from honor and status in one's own neighborhood.

Many Christians, however, were loath to give up the quest for a high place in the esteem of others. They wanted to have a function in society and desired economic, political, and social opportunities. Such individuals sought to accumulate some wealth and have some influence. But that was not going to happen unless they participated in the cultic feasts and in the temple prostitution. The letters to the churches in the book of Revelation indicate that some Christians weighed the options and asked, "Isn't John being just a little exclusive here? Doesn't God want us to evangelize the world? How can we reach the upper classes for Christ if we are not involved in their lives?"

So early Christians seem to have faced a tension between outreach and involvement in society, on the one hand, and faithfulness to the full counsel of God, on the other. No doubt many Christians pointed out the seventh commandment: "Thou shalt not commit adultery." On what basis, then, could a serious Christian even think about participating in cultic prostitution? I would like to suggest that some Christians found a theological justification for such activity in the writings of Paul, who argued that the state had authority to require certain things.

"Everyone must *submit himself to the governing authorities,* for there is no authority except that which God has established. *The authorities that exist have been established by God.* Consequently, he who rebels against the authority is rebelling against what God has instituted, and those who do so will bring judgments on themselves. For rulers hold no terror for those who do right, but for those who do wrong. Do you want to be free from fear of the one in authority? Then do what is right and he will commend you. For he is God's servant to do you good. But if you do wrong, be afraid, for he does not bear the sword for nothing. He is God's servant, an agent of wrath to bring punishment on the wrongdoer. Therefore, it is necessary to *submit to the authorities,* not only because of possible punishment but also *because of conscience.* This is also why you pay taxes, for the authorities are God's servants, who give their full time to governing. Give everyone what you owe him: If you owe taxes, pay taxes; if revenue, then revenue; if respect, then respect; if honor, then honor" (Rom. 13:1-7, NIV).

Might the Nicolaitans consider themselves as following Paul's counsel when they submitted to the requirements of civil religion? "[Pray] for kings and all those in authority, that we may live peaceful and quiet lives in all godliness and holiness. This is good and pleases God our Savior" (1 Tim. 2:2, 3, NIV). We are to pray for, obey, respect, and honor the authorities. I'm sure Paul would not have approved of cultic prostitution. In 1 Corinthians 8-10, however, Paul is fairly clear that eating food offered to idols is not a major issue in itself. For Paul, 40 years before the writing of Revelation, eating food offered to idols was a personal choice based on the situation. One suspects that sincere Christians who differed with the perspective of Revelation might have found encouragement in Paul's letters, whether or not they were reading them correctly.

John's Response to the Compromisers

The reality is that Paul's situation was quite different than John's. *Circumstances alter cases.* By the time of Revelation the appropriate response was: "No compromise. Those idols may be deaf and dumb, but behind every idol is Satan himself. If you honor the idol, you invite Satan into your life, and you will lose your place in heaven. So you basically have a choice: honor God and lose your place now or honor Satan and lose it later."

The book of Revelation recommends social, political, and economic withdrawal from society, if necessary, in order to be faithful to the instructions of Jesus. John takes a hard line with the believers that Paul did not feel necessary in his day. Evidently circumstances had altered in the 40 years between Paul's letters and the book of Revelation. Actions that would have been acceptable in the past were no longer so because of changing circumstances.

How does one persuade believers to take such a radical stance? First of all, the book of Revelation creates what some scholars call a "symbolic universe." The empire of Rome dominates the "universe" of everyday experience. But Revelation describes an empire that transcends that of Rome.

27

Reality involves more than the world we see. There is more to life than just the money, power, and the social opportunities of this world. The book of Revelation offered the Christians of Asia Minor a larger perspective: they were kings and priests in their own right. They had genuine dignity in the eyes of God. In giving up their status in the present world, they gained political and religious status that transcended even that conferred by Rome.

But it was more than a matter of being on the right side now. Jesus was coming soon, and the believer needed to be on the right side when He returned. So Revelation taught that the difficulties Christians face were part of God's plan and that their current lack of power and wealth would not last forever. They would not always lack access to gold, because one day they would walk on gold. Nor do they need to compromise with society, because the people of God were on the winning side. True, Rome could threaten your life, your status, and your earthly possessions, but God was even more powerful than the Empire itself. Ultimately, whom would you rather face: the wrath of Rome or the wrath of God? The message of Revelation was a no-compromise, hard-line one.

Applying Revelation to Our Day

The book of Revelation clearly had a powerful meaning for its original time and place. It would have created discussion all through the churches of Asia Minor. But the question remains: "What do we do with it today? Is the book of Revelation merely an ancient document that has nothing to say to the present? Or can it speak as powerfully in our day as it did in John's time? If so, how can we access that power today?"

Four Major Approaches

Traditionally, four schools of interpretation have sought to make the book of Revelation relevant to every succeeding generation: preterist, futurist, historicist, and idealist.

Preterist. The preterist school of interpretation suggests that John wrote the book of Revelation primarily for his day. Preterists believe that it offers no prophetic predictions of the future. It is simply a message from John to the Christian congregations of Asia Minor. If this is so, then we should study the book of Revelation along the same lines as the rest of the New Testament. From Matthew to Jude, we understand the New

Testament writings as messages to particular times and places, from which we can draw out truths that have ongoing relevance. Without question certain parts of Revelation, at least, fit such a description (Rev. 1:9-11; 22:16). But much of the book seems to call for a different approach.

Futurist. The futurist interpretation suggests that the book of Revelation almost solely focuses on the final crisis of earth's history. Rather than a message to the original audience, its relevance is primarily for the final generation. The popular theory of the rapture represents the major branch of futurism. But other forms of futurism are becoming increasingly popular even among Adventists. Does such a view of the book really fit sequences such as the seals and the trumpets? Is virtually the whole book intentionally limited to the final generation? Such a thesis needs to be proved rather than just assumed.

Historicist. The historicist mode of interpreting Revelation is the one most Adventists have grown up with. In one form or another, historicism portrays a sequence of history from the time of John until the Second Coming. This approach is grounded on the book of Daniel, in which you clearly find such historical sequences. But the historicist method also has its problems. If the book as a whole contains sequences of Christian history, then much of it doesn't apply directly to the point in time in which we now live. Historicists sometimes read the book as if the only point of spiritual value it has is in determining one's location in history. As a result, the historicist interpretation has often been extremely dry and left people hungry for real meaning in the book.

Idealist. The idealist approach suggests that the book of Revelation is not primarily historical, futurist, or even a message to the churches in John's day. Rather it contains timeless truths in symbolic form, principles that apply to any time and any place. Many Bible students often use this method in conjunction with the preterist approach. The interpreter explores how the original readers understood the book of Revelation, then seeks the broad and timeless principles that can apply to any age.

Which of the various schools of interpretation should we adopt? Do we have to choose? Well, for starters I should point out that the futurist and historicist approaches to Revelation only make sense if God truly inspired the book. Unless John is getting messages directly from God, he could not describe the future in detail as the historicist position suggests, nor the final days in detail, as futurism believes. Unless we accept the Bible as an inspired book, we could not take either of the two positions.

But if you believe in inspiration, all four approaches have validity. First, as we have seen, the book of Revelation certainly spoke powerfully to its original audience. So the preterists have a point. Second, the book claims to describe important events that are still future in our day—the Second Coming and even beyond. So a futurist approach to the book of Revelation will prove to be at least partly right. Third, the book of Revelation unquestionably describes the future from John's perspective (Rev. 1:1) and parts of it (such as Revelation 12), at least, portray a sequence of events from the prophet's day to the end of the world. So the historicist approach is likely to be helpful at various points in the book. Finally, the book of Revelation contains many themes applicable to any age. "Whoever has an ear, let him hear what the spirit says to the churches" (Rev. 2:7, etc.) So all four approaches have a certain amount of validity for studying the Apocalypse.

I do not believe that we should impose any particular viewpoint on Revelation like a template. A healthier approach is to go text by text and ask: "What is the approach called for in this passage?" As we go through the book of Revelation, we will want to be sensitive to the evidence of the text. We will let the biblical text govern what we see in the passage. In other words, we don't want to impose our ideas on Revelation, but let the text itself teach us how to understand it.

Balanced Christian Living

Does John's conflict with the Nicolaitans of Asia Minor offer us any lessons for today? In some ways our society echoes the time in which John lived. People do not appreciate exclusivism and consider comments such as "I have the truth" or "I belong to the true church" as out of line. It is natural these days to be inclusive. At the same time standards and certainties seem to be breaking down. Much of contemporary thinking concludes that everybody has some handle on truth and nobody has all the truth. But even though it may seem threatening to the standards and certainties of most churches, such a philosophy is not all bad. Isn't it true that we all have a lot to learn? That we all have a grasp on some aspect of ultimate truth? I believe that God is using the "postmodern" shift in today's world to bring us into a more balanced view of the Bible than may have been possible in a previous generation.

The postmodern outlook helps us to notice that Jesus and Paul support a more inclusive approach. They reached out to segments of society that no "respectable" religious person would have touched. As a result, they fellowshiped with Gentiles, prostitutes, and others that the larger society considered as outcasts. So the Nicolaitans of Asia Minor may have had a point. In order to reach Roman society it helped to be involved in at least some aspects of the general culture.

But the book of Revelation warns us that inclusion has its limits. Though outreach calls us to be all things to everyone (1 Cor. 9:19-23), we must not think, say, or do things that compromise our loyalty to God. Although we want to reach out to other people—although we want to be open to truth wherever we might find it—there come times in every Christian life when the only faithful answer is "No, absolutely not." At such times John insists that we are to shun compromise even if our very lives are at stake. To paraphrase Ecclesiastes: "There is a time to be inclusive and a time to be exclusive." John wrote Revelation at a time when the churches needed to say no.

So in the book of Revelation we discover messages of God to that time and that place, but we also encounter messages for our time and place. The New Testament, Revelation included, offers a message of balance. On the one hand, Christianity needs inclusiveness, to reach out to those we don't normally touch. On the other hand, it demands strong boundaries wherever inclusiveness would bring us in conflict with God's will. We can attain such balance best through a broad-based approach to Scripture. So in the next chapter we will take a quick survey of Bible prophecy from Genesis to Revelation. Out of this broad perspective we will gain principles that guide us to a healthy understanding of Revelation in all of its complexities.

---

[1] Adela Yarbro Collins, *Crisis and Catharsis: The Power of the Apocalypse* (Philadelphia: Westminster Press, 1984), pp. 84-104.

[2] *Ibid.,* p.101.

[3] The quotation is from Pliny *Epistulae* 96. Translated by Roland H. Bainton and quoted in Bainton, *Christendom: A Short History of Christianity and Its Impact on Western Civilization* (New York: Harper and Row, 1966), vol. 1, p. 57. Page 58 of the same book summarizes Trajan's response.

[4] Leonard L. Thompson, *The Book of Revelation: Apocalypse and Empire* (New York: Oxford University Press, 1990), pp. 95-115; G. K. Beale, *The Book of Revelation,* New International Greek Testament Commentary, edited by I. Howard Marshall and Donald A. Hagner (Grand Rapids: Eerdmans, 1999), pp. 5-16; and Kenneth A. Strand, Review of Leonard L. Thompson's "The Book of Revelation: Apocalypse and Empire" in *Andrews University Seminary Studies* 29 (1991): 188-190 support the traditional position.

2

THE PATTERNS
OF BIBLE PROPHECY

Prophets are making a comeback in today's world. The *National Enquirer* tabloid is full of them. Perhaps you've heard of Nostradamus, the sixteenth-century French physician and chef of Jewish heritage. Born to a father forced to convert to Catholicism around 1501, Nostradamus became renowned because of predictions that seemed to come true a short time after he made them. Emboldened by his success at predicting the near future, Nostradamus tried his hand at predicting major events extending through the next 2,000 years or so. He laid out his pre-dictions in 1,000 four-line poems, or quatrains, divided into "centuries" of a hundred each. Many of his predictions even contained specific dates.

The most famous of Nostradamus' dated predictions concerned the year 1999:

"The year 1999, seven months,

From the sky will come a great King of terror,

To resuscitate the great king of Angoulmois;

Before, after, Mars will reign by good luck."*

The language is clearly ambiguous. Many looked for its fulfillment in terms of a meteor shower or some other heavenly event. Most of these in-dividuals also anticipated that some significant conflict might break out during the year, if not in the month of July itself. But the date came and went, and people observed nothing that fit it.

In the mid–1960s I was aware of another alleged prophet named Jeane Dixon. She claimed to have insight into detailed future events. Two of her predictions seemed verifiable enough that I made note of them and watched for their fulfillment. One of them was that the unpopular views of Barry Goldwater (remember him?), a losing Republican candidate for the presidency in 1964, would be vindicated within the next decade. I'm not aware that it ever occurred. Another prediction of hers claimed that the scrapping of a miniature military missile project would prove to be a huge mistake by the end of the 1970s. As far as I know, no one ever missed the weapon. The concept of prophets is something we're used to. But successful prophets is another matter.

One of the first things you notice about the book of Revelation is its claim to be a written prophecy (Rev. 1:3 and 22:10). For those who know the Bible, that concept recalls the Old Testament which contains many examples of prophetic writings: Isaiah, Jeremiah, Ezekiel, Daniel, Zechariah, and Malachi, among others. The Bible offers many models of what prophecy is like. As we examine those models we gain a clearer understanding of how to read the prophecies of Revelation.

The exciting thing about the book of Revelation is that it makes a number of predictions about the future. Many of them still remain unfulfilled. This raises the question as to how we can accurately understand unfulfilled prophecies. What can we learn about our future from Revelation? How can we avoid the interpretive mistakes of the past? *The only safe way to interpret unfulfilled prophecy is to understand how prophecy was fulfilled in the past.* The Bible contains many prophecies that met their realization within the biblical context. As we study such completed prophecies, we can learn how to handle the unfulfilled prophecies of Revelation in a responsible way.

So in this chapter we will take a look at the patterns of Bible prophecy. As we do so we will observe *how* prophecy works throughout Scripture. We will see how the language used to describe the future compares to the actual events that correspond to that language. In this chapter we will not examine Revelation itself, but will instead discover the broad biblical groundwork for how we should understand the book. As we survey the entire biblical witness we will observe patterns of prophecy that continue in the book of Revelation.

Four Mighty Acts of God

When you look at the big picture of the Old Testament you discover that everything centers on four major acts of God: Creation, the Flood, the Exodus, and the return from Babylonian exile. Most of the prophecies in the Old Testament concerned one or more of these four great events. At first glance it may not appear that this has much to do with Revelation. It will, however, provide the foundation upon which we can base a sound understanding of Revelation. We will begin at the beginning.

Creation and the Flood

The original Hebrew of Genesis describes the Flood (Gen. 6-9) as an undoing of Creation (Gen. 1; 2). When you compare the two stories, you notice that the Flood is a piece by piece reversal of the creation. Then a re-creation that puts the world back together again follows the Flood. While this is obvious to the reader of the Hebrew you can also see much of it through a closer look at the English text.

In Creation, for example, God followed a process of separation and distinction. He used the atmosphere to divide the waters above from the waters below (Gen. 1:7), then separated the waters from the dry land (verse 9). And that's not all. "God saw that the light was good, and he separated the light from the darkness" (verse 4, NIV). "And God said, 'Let there be lights in the expanse of the sky to separate the day from the night, and let them serve as signs to mark seasons and days and years'" (verse 14, NIV). Separation and distinction, then, are the *how* of the creation process.

Now let's compare the previous texts with the way Genesis describes the Flood. "In the six hundredth year of Noah's life, on the seventeenth day of the second month—on that day all *the springs of the great deep burst forth, and the floodgates of the heavens were opened.* And rain fell on the earth forty days and forty nights" (Gen. 7:11, 12, NIV). According to this passage, the waters under the earth rose up and the waters above the earth poured down. What God had separated in the creation came together and that which was distinct became unified again. The Flood was a reversal of the separation and distinction that took place at Creation.

"The waters rose and covered the mountains to a depth of more than twenty feet" (verse 20, NIV). At Creation God separated the waters from the dry land. During the Flood those waters once again covered the dry land. In other words, the destruction of the Flood returns the earth to the condition it was in before Creation: "Now the earth was formless and empty, darkness was over the surface of the deep, and the Spirit of God was hovering over the waters" (Gen. 1:2, NIV; cf. 8:1). So the biblical author portrays the Flood as a bit by bit undoing of the Creation.

But Creation not only had its distinctions but also its unities. The unities included the relationship between Adam and God, between Adam and Eve, and between the human pair and their environment. The deluge story also reverses these unities. The Flood occurs because of a breakdown in the human relationship with God (Gen. 6:5-7, 12, 13). People also begin to hate and murder one another (Gen. 4:8, 23, 24; 6:13). The environment falls apart and the human ability to control it gets destroyed (Gen. 6:17; 7:10, 11, 23). So in the Flood story that which Creation made separate now comes together and that which was united gets torn apart.

The decisive point is this: the *language* of the Flood story is the language of the Creation. The Flood story utilizes the very same vocabulary and phrasing used in the description of the original Creation. Then when the destruction of the Flood ends and the waters have gone down, Genesis 8, 9 describes the re-creation of the world. "But God remembered Noah and all the wild animals and the livestock that were with him in the ark, and he sent a *wind* over the earth, and the waters receded" (Gen. 8:1, NIV).

With this "wind" (same Hebrew word as "spirit" in Genesis 1:2) the process of re-creation after the Flood began. The language of the re-creation parallels that of the original Creation. Once again the dry land appears (Gen. 8:13); God renews the seasons (verse 22); and the text speaks of human beings in the image of God (Gen. 9:6). And this time God guarantees the distinctions He has created: "I establish my covenant with you: Never again will all life be cut off by the waters of a flood; never again will there be a flood to destroy the earth" (verse 11, NIV).

What I hope is clear at this point is that the *language* of God's second mighty act—the Flood—parallels that of the first mighty act—the Creation. But the parallels do not end there. The biblical account describes Noah, the chief figure in the Flood story, as a "second Adam." At Creation God brought the animals to Adam, and in the Flood story He led the animals to Noah. "Pairs of all creatures that have the breath of life in them came to Noah and entered the ark" (Gen. 7:15, NIV). God also prescribes Noah's diet just as He did Adam's in the original creation. Note the similarity of language in the instructions that God gives to Adam and Noah:

Genesis 1:26-30, NIV	Gen 9:1-3, NIV
"Then God said, 'Let us make man in our image, in our likeness, and let them rule over *the fish of the sea and the birds of the air,* over the livestock, over all the earth, and over all *the creatures that move along the ground.'* . . . God blessed them and said to them, *'Be fruitful and increase in number;* fill the earth and subdue it. Rule over *the fish of the sea and the birds of the air* and over every living creature *that moves on the ground.'* Then God said, 'I give you every seed-bearing plant on the face of the whole earth and every tree that has fruit with seed in it. They will be *yours for food.* And to all *the beasts of the earth and all the birds of the air* and all the creatures *that move on the ground*—everything that has the breath of life in it—*I give every green plant for food.'* And it was so."	"Then God blessed Noah and his sons, saying to them, *'Be fruitful and increase in number* and fill the earth. The fear and dread of you will fall upon all *the beasts of the earth* and all *the birds of the air,* upon every *creature that moves along the ground,* and upon all *the fish of the sea;* they are given into your hands. Everything that lives and moves will be *food for you.* Just as *I gave you the green plants,* I now give you everything.'"

Scripture, therefore, portrays Noah as a second Adam, a new Adam. In fact, the very language of the Hebrew is parallel. The name "Adam" means "earth." Using the very same Hebrew term Genesis 9:20 says, "Noah, a man of the soil *[adamah],* proceeded to plant a vineyard (NIV)." Noah was a man of the earth. Was Adam a man of the earth? "And the Lord God formed the man from the dust of the ground and breathed into his nostrils the breath of life, and the man became a living being" (Gen. 2:7, NIV). Furthermore, just as Adam fell into sin and shame by eating from the fruit of a tree (Gen. 3:5-10), Noah shamed himself by drinking from the fruit of the vine (Gen. 9:20-23). Genesis says of Adam that when he ate the fruit, his eyes were opened (Gen.

3:5,7). As for Noah, after he became drunk, he awoke and realized what had happened to him (Gen. 9:24).

We find amazing and purposeful parallels between the story of Creation and the story of the Flood. When the biblical author describes the Flood, the text employs the language of Creation. And when Scripture depicts the new creation after the Flood, we again see the vocabulary of Creation used. In other words, God employed the language of the past to describe His working in the present:

Creation	The Flood
Waters cover earth	Waters cover earth
Spirit overshadows waters	Wind blows over waters
Waters divided	Ark passes through waters
Dry land appears	
Image of God	Dry land appears
Dominion over earth	Animals afraid of Noah
Fruitful and multiply	Fruitful and multiply
Adam	Second Adam (Noah)
Formed from the earth	Man of the soil
Put to sleep	
Woman formed	New earth formed
Shamed by fruit of tree	Shamed by fruit of vine
Paradise	
Tree of life	
Test	
Serpent	
Covenant implied	Covenant renewed

When you compare the two stories, it becomes evident that, in these two mighty acts, God was operating according to a consistent pattern. You could say that His actions in the Creation story foreshadowed His deeds during the time of the Flood. Since *God is consistent,* His past actions are predictive of His future ones.

But while the pattern between the two accounts is plain, differences do exist between the Flood and the Creation story. The Noah story has no serpent, no testing tree, nor a tree of life, and no woman plays a prominent role. So the Flood narrative does not repeat all the elements of the Creation story. God is consistent, but not mindlessly so. He uses the language of the past to describe His later actions, but the correspondence is not point by point. Thus while God is consistent, *He is not predictable.* We will see this pattern again in God's third mighty act of the Old Testament: the Exodus.

The Exodus Story

The Creation account begins with a formless earth covered by water (Gen. 1:2). The Flood story commences with the chaos of sin (Gen. 6:5-7) and then describes the earth's return to the condition it was in before Creation began (Gen. 1:2; 7:18-20; 8:1). But the Exodus story contains a significant difference. Instead of the waters covering the whole earth they are a limited body of water called the Red Sea. The waters aren't worldwide. So the story of the Exodus would at first glance seem to be very different from Creation or the Flood.

The Hebrew version of the Red Sea crossing, nevertheless, mirrors the vocabulary of both the Creation and the Flood. The use of such language is so clear that we can observe it even in English: "Then Moses stretched out his hand over the sea, and all that night the Lord drove the sea back with a strong east *wind* and turned it into *dry land.* The *waters were divided* and the Israelites went through the sea on *dry ground*, with a wall of water on their right and on their left" (Ex. 14:21, 22, NIV).

The biblical writer carefully chose the italicized words in the above passage to recall the account of Creation. The author could have selected other Hebrew words to describe the historical event in an accurate way. But the vocabulary employed specifically and intentionally reminds us of the Creation. "Now the earth was formless and empty, darkness was over the surface of the deep, and the *Spirit* of God was hovering over the waters" (Gen. 1:2, NIV). In the Hebrew, the word for "spirit" and the word for "wind" are the same. A "wind from God" moves over the waters in the original creation and a "wind from God" sweeps over the waters of the Red Sea. The result in both cases is that the "waters were divided"—the same Hebrew language as in Genesis 1:6, 7.

Exodus 14 also tells us that the Israelites went through the sea on "dry ground." The author could have chosen many Hebrew words to present the fact. The actual word used in Exodus 14 is the same word employed in Genesis 1 to refer to the dry land of the original creation (Gen. 1:9, 10). Since other Hebrew words could have been used to depict the Exodus, the author clearly interprets the Exodus as a mighty act of God according to the pattern of the Creation (and also the Flood). In other words, God uses the language of Creation and the Flood to portray the Exodus.

Having observed the pattern, we begin to see many other parallels between the Exodus and God's previous acts. "Then say to Pharaoh, 'This is what the Lord says: Israel is my firstborn son'" (Ex. 4:22, NIV). Who was God's firstborn son in terms of the whole human race? Adam. But in Exodus 4 God describes the whole nation of Israel as his firstborn son. Just as the original Adam had dominion over the earth (Gen. 1:26, 28), Israel receives the dominion over the land of Canaan (Ex. 6:4; Lev. 25:38).

And just as God created Adam and Eve in the original Creation, so now He creates a people—Israel. In the original garden God gave Adam and Eve a tree of life to keep them alive and healthy (Gen. 2:9; 3:22), and in the Exodus story God provides the equivalent of the tree of life. He uses miraculous bread (manna, Ex. 16) to sustain them in the wilderness. Finally, just as the tree of knowledge of good and evil tested Adam (Gen 2:15-17; 3:3, 11-13), in the Exodus story He tested His people several times to see if they would be faithful to Him (Ex. 16:4; 20:20; Deut. 8:2, 16).

"Remember how the Lord your God led you all the way in the desert these forty years, to humble you and to test you in order to know what was in your heart, whether or not you would keep his commands. He humbled you, causing you to hunger and then feeding you with manna, which neither you nor your fathers had known, to teach you that man does not live on bread alone but on every word that comes from the mouth of the Lord" (Deut. 8:2, 3, NIV).

We can observe still other parallels. Just as both Eden and the wilderness had a test, so also both contained a serpent (Gen. 3:1ff.; Num. 21:5-9). God made covenants with the original Adam and with Noah (Gen. 1:26-30, cf. Gen. 9:1-3), and He also established a covenant with Israel (Ex. 19, 20). Parallel after parallel exists between the work of God in the Exodus story and His activity in the Creation story and the Flood story.

But once again we observe some differences between the accounts. The Exodus account, in many ways, is a spiritualization of features in the

Creation	The Flood	The Exodus
Chaos	Chaos	Spiritual chaos
Waters cover earth	Waters cover earth	Red Sea
Spirit overshadows waters	Wind blows over waters	Wind blows over waters
Waters divided	Ark passes through waters	Waters divided
Dry land appears	Dry land appears	Dry land appears
Image of God		First born
Dominion over earth	Animals afraid of Noah	Dominion over Canaan
Fruitful and multiply	Fruitful and multiply	As the sands of the sea
Adam	Second Adam (Noah)	Creation of a people
Formed from the earth	Man of the soil	Land of Canaan
Put to sleep		
Woman formed	New earth formed	
Shamed by fruit of tree	Shamed by fruit of vine	
Paradise		Canaan
Tree of life		Manna
Test		Test in wilderness
Serpent		Serpent
Covenant implied	Covenant renewed	Covenant

Creation and Flood accounts. For example, the chaos of the waters around the earth is parallel not only to the Red Sea but also to the slavery of the Israelites. The Israelite situation was a spiritual mess (Ex. 1:8-22). They needed God's creative power to get them out of Egypt (Ex. 3:7-10). So the chaos of Israel's condition was a spiritual one. The story of the Exodus *spiritualizes the literal things of the Creation* to show the consistency of God's actions in both accounts. The counterpart of Adam and Eve is Israel. The Garden of Eden becomes Canaan or Palestine. In the Exodus God leads them to a land flowing with milk and honey, well watered, like the Garden of Eden (Ex. 3:8,17; Num. 13:27).

As was the case with the Flood story, not all the details of the original Creation get repeated in the Exodus account. The wedding of Adam and Eve (Gen. 2:23-25; 4:1), the tree of knowledge of good and evil (Gen. 2:9, 16, 17; 3:11), the sleep of Adam that resulted in the creation of Eve (Gen. 2:21, 22), and the creation of sun, moon and stars (Gen. 1:14-19) are all elements of the Creation story that seem to find no parallel in the Exodus.

At the same time, the Exodus story contains new details that set the stage for later works of God. Moses, as a child, escapes from Pharaoh's attempts to kill him (Ex. 2:1-10; cf. Matt. 2:13-18). The blood of the Passover saves him along with the people of Israel (Ex. 12:1-30; 1 Cor. 5:7). God tests the Israelites for 40 years in the wilderness (Num. 14:34-35; Matt. 4:1-10). Adam and Eve don't themselves pass through the divided waters of the Creation (Gen. 1:7-9), but Israel actually passes through the divided waters. And the Exodus narrative actually contains two dividings of the waters—the first when they journey through the Red Sea and the second at the Jordan River. So we see in the Exodus account some fascinating similarities and differences with the original accounts of Creation and the Flood. While God's saving actions follow a clear pattern, He is not mindlessly tied to it.

Learning From the Pattern

I would encourage you to put the above observations to the test. Look up the texts I have listed along the way. Then read the books of Genesis and Exodus through for yourself. Compare the stories of God's three mighty acts. Can you see how the biblical writer takes up language from one story to the next?

So what can we learn from this series of patterns? What does this study have to do with prophecy? And in particular, what relevance does it have for the book of Revelation? I believe that five major insights about God have emerged from our brief study of the Creation, the Flood, and the Exodus. They provide a major key to opening the prophecies of Revelation.

1. **God is consistent.** His past actions foretell what He will do in His later actions. What He did at the Creation sets the pattern for what He did at the Red Sea. The two events are very different and yet the same God is at work in both instances. What He does now reminds us of what He did then. And what He is doing now points to what He will do later on. He is faithful to His promises. You can count on God, because He is consistent. But we need to qualify this insight by a second one.

2. **God is not predictable.** While God is consistent, sometimes He surprises us. You have to let God be God. He follows a definite pattern in the way He approaches people, events, and circumstances, but His later ac-

tivities do not carry out every detail of the model. God's consistency is not a mindless, point-by-point one. Sometimes people assume that He must carry out every detail of His past in exactly the same way in the future. So they assume that in unfulfilled prophecies God will do in minute detail exactly what He has said. But we must be careful not to put Him in a box. We must allow him His creative freedom. According to the Bible, God's later activity carries out much of the pattern—but not *all* of it.

3. **God is creative.** His later actions, while following the general pattern of His earlier ones, often enhance them, developing them more fully. God's revelation of Himself grows as His people become able to grasp it. The antitype doesn't just carry out the type as a point by point correspondence. God can transcend what He has done before. He is not limited to the details of His previous patterns.

When you compare prophecy and fulfillment in the Bible, therefore, you discover a creative God who operates freely within the limits of His overall consistency. He is not bound to carry out every detail, neither is He hindered from introducing something new. Sometimes a prophecy that He could have fulfilled in one way at one point in time He will actually bring to completion in a different way at a different time. Circumstances alter cases. As time moves on, we find God operating in creative ways to fulfill His word.

4. **God meets people where they are.** Whenever God reveals Himself, He does so within the time, place, and circumstances of the one who receives the revelation. As God speaks to prophets, He does so in their own *vocabulary,* language they have learned naturally from their own past. And, frankly, could prophets understand a message from God if they received it in a language they could not understand? Of course not.

You see, language is based on the sum total of our past experience. The only language we know is what we learn from babyhood on up. A 2-year-old toddles around and hears somebody say "appreciate." The child files that sound away for a couple of weeks and then encounters it again. By the third or fourth time, the toddler begins to have a sense of what that word means through its context and the way people generally express it. So the *language* that we all speak is the vocabulary of our own personal past. That is why God spoke to the writers of the Bible in the terminology and experiences of their past. God's revelations always come within the time, place, and circumstances in which the recipients lived.

The point I am getting at is that language is more than just Spanish, French, English, and Swahili. Even those who speak English have vast differences in the way they define things and the way their culture expresses itself. The English of the baby boomer is quite different from the English of the postmodern young person. So even though they may speak the same language, each person's unique experience affects what and how they understand. The soundest way to apply unfulfilled prophecy, then, is to interpret its meaning in terms of its original language and setting. If you want to understand Revelation, therefore, the soundest way to approach the book is in the language of John's past—language as he would have grasped it around A.D. 95.

The biblical evidence, however, tells us that "reading Revelation as if it were written to our time and place is not appropriate for the study of an ancient book in which God meets writers where they are. We should not approach the biblical book as if John was familiar with Ellen White. Nor should we read Revelation as if the author had studied *The Seventh-day Adventist Bible Commentary*. The message God has placed for us in the book of Revelation will be found in the language and perspective of the original situation in which God met John.

5. **There is a spiritualization of the biblical type.** Beginning with the Exodus event, we see a spiritualization of some of the types. In other words, the language of God's successive actions alters from literal to spiritual, or symbolic (from Flood to slavery, for example). It also shifts from global to more localized (from worldwide Flood to Red Sea). God can use the vocabulary of the past in literal terms at times (as in the Flood story's reminiscences of Creation), but He can also employ the same language to describe something more spiritual and more local (as in the account of the Exodus). The basic scenario and language gets repeated, but He uses that vocabulary in a figurative, spiritualized form, moving from Adam to Israel or from Eden to Palestine. Scripture employs the same language but the meaning of the words now expands in a spiritual way.

Recognizing the patterns in God's activity is vital for our study of the book of Revelation. As we see how God fulfilled the promises and prophecies of the past, we gain a clearer picture of His workings in our present and future. And as we move toward the book of Revelation, we will next examine the Old Testament prophets, whose writings span from

Isaiah to Malachi in the Bible. We will find the five principles we have developed further confirmed by this next stage of God's dealings with His people Israel.

The New Exodus

Should you read the Bible through from Isaiah to Malachi you would discover that the major theme running through the prophets is Judah's exile to Babylon and subsequent return. If the pattern we have seen so far continues in the prophets, what language would the prophets use to describe the Exile? That of the Exodus, God's mightiest act of deliverance from captivity. God would work in the captivity to Babylon as He did in the Egyptian captivity. So when the prophets write about the Exile, they do so in terms of the Exodus. They describe the return from exile as a "New Exodus." God plans to repeat the Exodus all over again. To put it another way, *God is consistent.*

Hosea. Let's begin our study of this New Exodus with the earliest of the writing prophets. Hosea prophesied around 750 B.C. (Another biblical prophet who wrote during this time was Amos.) The Israel of David and Solomon had tragically split apart, producing two nations—Israel and Judea—where there had formerly been only one. While the dual kingdoms never returned to the full glory of Solomon's reign, the time of Hosea found both at the height of their prosperity. Jereboam II was king in Israel, and of all the northern Israelite kings, he was probably the most powerful and successful (2 Kings 14:23-29). But when God's people become prosperous they tend to forget that it is His blessing that enables people to get wealth. That's what happened to Israel.

"She [Israel] has not acknowledged that I was the one
who gave her the grain, the new wine and oil,
who lavished on her the silver and gold—
which they used for Baal" (Hosea 2:8, NIV).

In its prosperity Israel overlooked who had provided that wealth. Israel did not remember who commanded the rain to water the earth to provide the grain, the new wine, and the oil. Instead of serving God with the abundance He had given them, Israel used its wealth to turn away from Him. The Lord decided to respond by removing the luxury that had become an obstacle to Israel's relationship with Him.

" 'Therefore I will take away my grain when it ripens,
　　and my new wine when it is ready.
I will take back my wool and my linen,
　　intended to cover her nakedness.
So now I will expose her lewdness
　　　　before the eyes of her lovers;
　　no one will take her out of my hands.
I will stop all her celebrations:
　　her yearly festivals,
　　her New Moons,
　　her Sabbath days—
　　all her appointed feasts.
I will ruin her vines and her fig trees,
　　which she said were her pay from her lovers;
I will make them a thicket,
　　and wild animals will devour them.
I will punish her for the days
　　she burned incense to the Baals;
　　she decked herself with rings and jewelry,
　　and went after her lovers,
　　but me she forgot,'
　　　　declares the Lord" (verses 9-13, NIV).

God here describes the future exile that Israel would experience. At that time He would take away the grain, new wine, oil, technology, everything—even their feasts, Temple services, and worship. All these would vanish when they went into exile. Because they had forsaken God, He does not intervene to stop the nation's decline and fall. But good news mingles in with the bad. God sends them into exile, not as a final rejection, but in order to win them back.

"Therefore I am now going to *allure* her;
　　I will lead her into the desert
　　　　and speak tenderly to her.
I will give her back her vineyards,
　　　　and will make the Valley of Achor a door of hope.
There she will sing as in the days of her youth,
　　as in the day she came up out of Egypt" (verses 14-15, NIV).

46

Notice the word "allure." God seeks a relationship with Israel in terms of the eagerness with which a young man might court a young woman. What desert is he talking about here? The desert of Sinai. God is recalling the Exodus, an earlier stage in His relationship with Israel. Family counselors tell us that any time a marriage is in trouble, the best thing to do is to remember the early attentions—go back to the activities, conversations, and relationships that put you in love in the first place. As you renew the early attentions, love often returns in force. So God here is describing His relationship with Israel as that between a husband and a wife. The Exodus from Egypt was like a courtship stage in which God fell in love with Israel and Israel fell in love with Him. So when the relationship comes to a crisis, as recounted in Hosea, God remembers the Exodus from Egypt, the time of courtship and first love.

If Israel wishes to turn away from Him, however, God will allow her to go her own way. He will agree to the divorce. But He won't let it end there. Instead, God is going to start all over again and court her as if they were just meeting for the first time! He will bring her back to the place where they first fell in love—the wilderness of Sinai. And He will do everything in His power to restore the relationship to an even better condition than before.

Here's the point that is significant for us. In Hosea's prophecy of the Exile and the return He uses the language of the Exodus, the vocabulary of Egypt and the wilderness. We find no hint here of Babylon or the Euphrates River. In other words, God describes the exile to Babylon in terms of the Exodus from Egypt. *He employs the language of the past to describe the future.*

So we can add a sixth principle of prophetic interpretation to the five that we discovered earlier in this chapter. When the writing prophets of the Old Testament speak of the Exile and of the return from Babylon, they tend to speak in the language of the Exodus. But here Scripture does not employ the language of the past to describe the present, rather it uses that language to portray the future. God prophesies the Exile in the language of the Exodus. Or to put it more generally: *Prophets use the language of the past to depict the future.*

Micah. A contemporary of Hosea was the prophet Micah. He prophesied to the kingdom of Judah (just to the south) a short time after the prophecy recorded in Hosea 2. He too follows the pattern that we noticed in Hosea. In discussing the Exile he speaks in the language of the Exodus.

"As in the days when you came out of Egypt,
    I will show them my wonders.
Nations will see and be ashamed,
    deprived of all their power.
They will lay their hands on their mouths
    and their ears will become deaf.
They will lick dust like a snake,
    like creatures that crawl on the ground.
They will come trembling out of their dens;
    they will turn in fear to the Lord our God
        and will be afraid of you.
Who is a God like you,
    who pardons sin and forgives the transgression
        of the remnant of his inheritance?
You do not stay angry forever
    but delight to show mercy.
You will *again* have compassion on us;
    you will tread our sins underfoot
    and hurl all our iniquities into the depths of the sea.
You will be true to Jacob,
    and show mercy to Abraham,
    as you pledged on oath to our fathers
        in days long ago" (Micah 7:15-20, NIV).

Did you notice the word "again" in the above passage? "You will again have compassion on us." "Again" combined with "as in the days when you came out of Egypt" makes it clear that the prophet has in mind a "New Exodus" modeled on the first Exodus out of Egypt.

The principle of "spiritualizing the type" is very strong in this passage. The New Exodus will be as much spiritual as literal. God's purpose for it is to forgive His people and to restore their hearts to Him. He's not primarily interested in having a nation with political power on His side but rather in a spiritual relationship with His people. Not satisfied with merely a "name" relationship, He wants a heart relationship of genuine intimacy. In that sense the New Exodus will transcend the previous one.

So Micah 7 also describes the Exile and return in terms of a New Exodus. But instead of the Red Sea, he talks about the "depths of the sea." For him the sea is not a physical barrier that God will physically divide, but the place where His people leave their sins behind. Micah prophesies that they will discard their sins and transgressions in Babylon, and when they come back home, they are going to be faithful to God. So the prophecy of the Exile builds on the language of the Exodus in a spiritual way.

Isaiah. Isaiah prophesied just a few years after Hosea and Micah. He too describes the Exile in the language of the Exodus.

"The Lord will dry up the gulf of the Egyptian sea;
    with a scorching wind he will sweep his hand
        over the Euphrates River.
He will break it up into seven streams
    so that men can cross over in sandals.
There will be a highway for the remnant of his people
    that is left from Assyria,
as there was for Israel
    when they came up from Egypt" (Isa. 11:15, 16, NIV).

Here the Euphrates River functions as a parallel to the Red Sea of the Exodus. A highway of return from Assyria would cross over the Euphrates River. When Israel comes out of captivity it will go through the Euphrates River in a manner similar to the way Israel passed through the Red Sea.

Do you remember the principle that *God is consistent?* What He did for His people in Egypt, He will do again when they return from the Exile. Isaiah uses the language of the past to depict the future. But that isn't all that is going on here. While we can describe the Exile in terms of the Exodus *God is not bound to the entire pattern.* Did Israel actually return from Assyria? No. By the time of the Exile, Israel no longer existed. Only Judah remained. Assyria had also been destroyed and Babylon had become the new superpower. Not only that, did the remnant of God's people actually pass through the Euphrates River in sandals? No, bridges spanned the Euphrates River right in the city of Babylon. How do you explain the anomalies in this prophecy? *God meets people where they are.* At the time Isaiah was written, Israel had not yet been destroyed and Assyria still ruled the territory of Babylon. So He gave the prophecy in the context of the time, place, and circumstances of Isaiah's day. When the fulfillment came circumstances had altered the case.

The Euphrates River did dry up, however. That happened when Cyrus, king of Persia, surrounded Babylon. Since the city's walls seemed too difficult to take by siege Cyrus tried to find some way to get around its defenses. He did that by diverting the Euphrates River—drying up its waters—and marching his soldiers along the river bed, under the walls, and into the city. In principle the Exodus happened again, but many details were different this time. *God is consistent, but He is not predictable. He meets people where they are* at each stage of the historical drama.

Another text in Isaiah takes a slight turn from the previous one. It begins with the language of the Exodus again, but then shifts to something new.

"This is what the Lord says—

he who made *a way through the sea,*
a path through the mighty waters,
who drew out *the chariots and horses,*
the army and reinforcements together,
and they lay there, never to rise again,
extinguished, snuffed out like a wick:
'Forget the former things;
do not dwell on the past.
See, I am doing a new thing!
Now it springs up; do you not perceive it?
I am making a way in the desert
and streams in the wasteland'" (Isa. 43:16–19, NIV).

In this passage the Exodus still provides the model for the return from exile. We find references to passing through the waters and the destruction of chariots, horses, and armies. But the event to come is also something that will transcend the Exodus. The past provides the language for the future, but once again *God is creative* and the fulfillment is not bound to the pattern in every detail.

I am emphasizing these principles because they provide the basis for making a sound analysis of unfulfilled prophecies. Many people treat unfulfilled prophecy as if written directly to them and to their own time and circumstances. They forget that when God gave the prophecy He did not use the language of their day but that of the prophet's past. I cannot underestimate the importance of this principle. *When you study a book such as Revelation, the content concerns the prophet's future, but the vocabulary belongs to the prophet's past. We should not expect a point by point correspondence between every detail of the prophecy and its fulfillment.*

Another passage from the book of Isaiah, one often used in conjunction with the book of Revelation, illustrates this point.

"Behold, *I will create new heavens*
    and a new earth.
The former things will not be remembered,
    nor will they come to mind.
But *be glad and rejoice forever*
    in what I will create,
      for I will create Jerusalem to be a delight
        and its people a joy.
I will rejoice over Jerusalem
    and take delight in my people;
the sound of weeping and of crying
    will be heard in it no more" (Isa. 65:17-19, NIV).

Most people assume the passage describes our future. In fact, the book of Revelation actually uses the text to speak about the New Jerusalem that God has prepared for His people. But here in Isaiah, God refers to the Exile and the Return. Some of the language has taken on an extended meaning over time (confirmed by inspiration), but when Isaiah writes he has in mind the Exile and the Return. If you read the chapter in context, you will see that it doesn't discuss eternal life in heaven, but rather people living longer lives on this earth.

"Never again will there be in it
    an infant who lives but a few days,
    or an old man who does not live out his years;
he who dies at a hundred
    will be thought a mere youth;
he who fails to reach a hundred
    will be considered accursed" (verse 20, NIV).

This is not a description of heaven the way the Revelator sees it (Rev. 21:4)! Heaven as we understand it doesn't include death. But as a depiction of the mighty things God plans to do when they return from Exile, the text makes sense. In other places Isaiah has described the Exile in the vocabulary of the Exodus. But aspects of God's future mighty act are so great that Scripture can only portray them in the vocabulary of Creation. Remember the principle of *spiritualizing the type?* Using the language of Creation doesn't mean that Isaiah is describing the very end of earth's history—the account of the Exodus also employed creation language (Ex. 14:21, 22). In this case the vocabulary of creation depicts what will take place after the exile to Babylon.

Daniel. You may be thinking, *OK. I see your point when it comes to Isaiah. But isn't Revelation an apocalyptic book, more like Daniel? Surely in these types of books the prophet speaks directly about the future. He's not addressing his time and place but ours. Shouldn't we read those books differently than the other prophets?* A fair question. But a look at the evidence suggests that even apocalyptic passages such as Daniel 7 *use the language of the past to talk about the future.* Daniel's vision portrays the sequence of future kingdoms in the vocabulary of Creation.

"Daniel said, 'In my vision at night I looked, and there before me were the four winds of heaven churning up the great sea'" (Dan. 7:2, NIV). Does the imagery of the winds blowing over the sea sound familiar? We've seen similar language already in Genesis 1:2. The vision of Daniel 7 begins with an echo of the chaotic waters before Creation. Then after Daniel's depiction of a series of animals we come to a fascinating statement in verses 13 and 14:

"In my vision at night I looked, and there before me was one *like a son of man,* coming with the clouds of heaven. He approached the Ancient of Days and was led into his presence. He was given authority, glory and sovereign power; *all peoples, nations and men* of every language worshiped him. *His dominion is an everlasting dominion* that will not pass away, and his kingdom is one that will never be destroyed" (NIV).

The italicized language reminds us of Adam's dominion over the creatures of the earth (Gen. 1:26-28), an authority that he exercised when he named the animals (Gen. 2:19, 20). So Daniel 7, as in the case of other Old Testament prophets, applies the language of Creation to the prophet's future: winds churning up the sea, animals appearing, and a son of man (a second Adam) who receives dominion over these animals. Thus Daniel 7 describes the future history of the world as a new creation of God. Once again *Scripture takes the language of the past to speak about the future.*

What excites me about this reading of Daniel 7 is that this prophecy made perfect sense when Daniel was writing. God's people were right in the middle of the Exile at that time, captives in Babylon. How would the prophet view the animals in Daniel 7? They represented the nations who were oppressing the people of God. The vision portrays these nations as vicious, ravenous beasts.

So what was the message of the vision to Daniel and his people? Something like this: "Just as Adam had dominion over the animals after Creation, so the Son of man will have dominion over these nations that are oppressing you and your people." The meaning of Daniel 7, in other words, was that God was still in control. The world seemed chaotic because wicked nations were doing evil things to the people of God. But His people were not to be discouraged. Despite all appearances, the Lord had not lost control of the situation.

Remember the principle that *God meets people where they are?* We see that very clearly in Daniel 7. God gives a message to Daniel about the future of the world. But His purpose was also to assure the prophet that He was in control of present circumstances as well. In Daniel 2 Nebuchadnezzar, the king of Babylon, had a vision similar to Daniel's with a parallel interpretation. But it had one major difference. Nebuchadnezzar's dream symbolized the nations of the world by an idol. That makes sense because Nebuchadnezzar was a pagan king. To him the nations represented shining examples of the gods they worshiped. The nations were something to be excited about. But to Daniel those same nations were vicious, ravenous beasts who were hurting his people. God gave the same message to each "prophet" in terms they would understand. *When God reveals the future, He does so through the language of the prophet's past. God meets people where they are.* We should not, therefore, expect point by point fulfillment of every detail, even in apocalyptic prophecy.

Further Examples of Prophetic Fulfillment
After the Return From Exile

What actually happened when Israel came back from Babylon? When compared to the texts we've been reading, the fulfillment was disappointing. But remember principle 2: *God is not predictable*. Many residents of Israel and Judah must have read the prophecies of Hosea, Micah, Isaiah, and others. I can imagine them making out charts to outline in advance just what God was going to do. But His work, when it came, wasn't quite what the predictors expected.

"On the twenty-first day of the seventh month,
the word of the Lord came through the prophet Haggai:
'Speak to Zerubbabel son of Shealtiel, governor of Judah,
to Joshua son of Jehozadak, the high priest,
and to the remnant of the people.
Ask them, *"Who of you is left who saw this house in its former glory?*
How does it look to you now?
Does it not seem to you like nothing?
But now be strong, O Zerubbabel,"
declares the Lord.
"Be strong, O Joshua son of Jehozadak,
the high priest.
Be strong, all you people of the land,"
declares the Lord,
"and work.
For I am with you,"
declares the Lord Almighty.
"This is what I covenanted with you
when you came out of Egypt.
And my Spirit remains among you. Do not fear."
'This is what the Lord Almighty says:
"In a little while I will once more shake the heavens and the earth,
the sea and the dry land.
I will shake all nations,
and the desired of all nations will come,
and *I will fill this house with glory,"*
says the Lord Almighty.
"The silver is mine and the gold is mine,"
declares the Lord Almighty.
"The glory of this present house
will be greater than the glory of the former house,"

says the Lord Almighty.
"And in this place I will grant peace,"
declares the Lord Almighty'" (Haggai 2:1-9, NIV).

In this passage the Lord notes their disappointment as they view the fulfillment of the prophecies of return from exile. Yet He affirms that it is a true fulfillment even though they have reason to question it. That's something to keep in mind as we approach unfulfilled prophecy—including the book of Revelation. From Münster to Waco people have tried to use the material in Revelation to gain a detailed knowledge of the future that God did not design for them to have. We all need to be reminded that *the same God who is consistent is not predictable.*

As time went on it gradually became clear that God's returning His people from the Babylonian Exile was not going to be the final event of earth's history. Attention more and more shifted to His greatest act of all—the arrival of the Messiah. But that raises a fresh question. Many people assume that the messianic prophecies of the Old Testament have more of a point-by-point fulfillment than the prophecies we have been looking at. Is this really so? Are the messianic prophecies of the Old Testament an exception to the rule that God uses the language of the past to describe events in the future? Are the messianic prophecies *more predictable* than the general trend? Let's look at a few examples.

The Messianic Prophecies

"'The days are coming,' declares the Lord,
'when *I will raise up to David a righteous Branch,*
a King who will reign wisely
and do what is just and right in the land.
In his days Judah will be saved
and Israel will live in safety.
This is the name by which he will be called:
The Lord Our Righteousness'" (Jer. 23:5, 6, NIV).

What do we learn from this text? First, the Messiah is coming, and He will be a king like David. David's kingship provides a historical model for what the Messiah will be like, an example of wise and just rulership. But obviously not every action of David provides a model for the righteous Messiah. The Messiah will be like David, but his life will

55

not be an exact replay of David's reign. Thus the line from prophecy to fulfillment here is not totally predictable.

A second aspect to this prophecy appears in the title given to the Messiah: "The Lord Our Righteousness." The king reigning in Judah at the time when Jeremiah gave his prophecy went by the name of Zedekiah, which in Hebrew means, "the Lord is my righteousness." Jeremiah tells us that the Messiah, when He comes, will be a king like Zedekiah. While Zedekiah did not live up to his own name, that name still served as a model of what the Messiah would be like. The Messiah would play the role that Zedekiah was supposed to fulfill. He would be the one who perfectly carried out the righteousness of God. So the messianic prophecy of Jeremiah 23 uses the language of the past and the present to project an image of what Messiah would be like in the future.

Let's go back to another prophecy in Isaiah:

"Again the Lord spoke to Ahaz, 'Ask the Lord your God for a sign, whether in the deepest depths or in the highest heights.' But Ahaz said, 'I will not ask; I will not put the Lord to the test.' Then Isaiah said, 'Hear now, you house of David! Is it not enough to try the patience of men? Will you try the patience of my God also? Therefore the Lord himself will give you a sign: *The virgin will be with child and will give birth to a son, and will call him Immanuel.* He will eat curds and honey when he knows enough to reject the wrong and choose the right. *But before the boy knows enough to reject the wrong and choose the right, the land of the two kings you dread will be laid waste'*" (Isa. 7:10-16, NIV).

This prophecy is talking about a king named Ahaz and a prophet named Isaiah. Ahaz is worried about two nations seeking to conquer his kingdom. Isaiah offers him a sign from the Lord. God sends him a message that a young woman (the Hebrew can be read either as "a young woman" or "a virgin") will conceive and have a child. The good news for Ahaz is that before the child is ready to eat solid food and before he knows right from wrong, the two nations will be destroyed. So this prophecy of the Messiah grows out of an immediate situation. God uses the language of the present to speak about the future. In the time of the Messiah God will deliver His people just as He did Ahaz in Isaiah's day (Isa. 9:1-7).

In Zechariah, a small book at the end of the Old Testament, we see the same principle operating again:

"Rejoice greatly, O Daughter of Zion!
    Shout, Daughter of Jerusalem!
  See, *your king comes to you,*
      righteous and having salvation,
      gentle and riding on a donkey,
      on a colt, the foal of a donkey.
  I will take away the chariots from Ephraim
      and the war-horses from Jerusalem,
      and the battle bow will be broken.
  He will proclaim peace to the nations.
      His rule will extend from sea to sea
      and from the River to the ends of the earth" (Zech. 9:9, 10, NIV).

Here we see references to Ephraim, Jerusalem, and the Euphrates (referred to just as "the River" in the text), language from the prophets's time and place, coupled with a description of the Messiah. But using such texts, could anyone have predicted the exact course of Jesus' life? No. Should it surprise us that some understood these same texts to predict that the Messiah would be a powerful king who would dominate the political forces in His world? Even Jesus' own disciples, after copious hints, failed to understand His Messiahship until Pentecost. Only after having known Jesus, walked with Him, and received God's interpretation through the Spirit, could anyone have fully understood how the life of Jesus was the fulfillment of these very prophecies.

The New Testament

This leads us to a seventh important principle of Bible prophecy that Jesus stated a couple times: "I have told you now before it happens, so that when it does happen you will believe" (John 14:29, NIV; cf. 13:19). Did Jesus say, "I'll tell you ahead of time so that you will know the future in advance? In fact, I'll help you make a chart that lines up all the events so that you can spot your place in history at all times"?

No, He did not. He *was* saying, however, that if you pay careful attention to His words, you will recognize the time of fulfillment *when* it comes, not before. When the prophesied events occur, you will discern them and the fulfillment will be clear. It was clear that Jesus was the fulfillment of the messianic prophecies once He had lived His life out. But the prophecies did not allow people to predict the exact course of His life in advance. *God is not predictable.* That means that *prophetic fulfillments are best recognized after they happen, not before.*

When it comes to uncompleted prophecy, a little tentativeness is advisable. It was the lack of such caution that led David Koresh to destruction. He thought he knew exactly what God wanted him to do and exactly how to bring about the result that the Lord had in mind. But he was wrong. It is critical that we search the Word to gain an understanding of unfulfilled prophecy. At the same time we need to maintain a sanctified tentativeness about our conclusions. We must allow God the freedom to be God.

The book of Revelation continues the pattern that we have seen all the way back to Genesis. When John wrote his book the events described in it were almost entirely future. Yet the basic language of the book of Revelation is that of John's past. Revelation is filled with the Old Testament. For example, notice the latter part of Revelation 13:

"And he performed great and miraculous signs, even causing *fire to come down from heaven to earth* in full view of men. Because of the signs he was given power to do on behalf of the first beast, he *deceived* the inhabitants of the earth" (Rev 13:13, 14, NIV).

At the time of the Exodus Pharaoh's magicians deceived him by using magical arts. The text in Revelation 13 also recalls how Elijah brought fire down from heaven to earth on Mount Carmel.

"He ordered them to *set up an image* in honor of the beast who was wounded by the sword and yet lived. He was given power to give breath to the image of the first beast, so that it could speak and *cause all who refused to worship the image to be killed*" (verses 14, 15, NIV).

The passage reminds us of Daniel 3 in which Nebuchadnezzar set up an image and threatened to kill anyone who refused to bow down and worship it.

"He also forced everyone small and great, rich and poor, free and slave, to receive a mark *on his right hand or on his forehead,* so that no one could buy or sell unless he had the mark, which is the name of the beast or the number of his name" (verses 16, 17, NIV).

In Deuteronomy 6 God tells the people to wear the Ten Commandments on the forehead and the hand. So the mark is in some way a counterfeit of the Ten Commandments. In order to make sense of the mark of the beast, you have to understand the Old Testament background—the language of the past that John was using.

"This calls for wisdom. If anyone has insight, let him calculate the number of the beast, for it is man's number. His number is 666" (Rev. 13:18, NIV).

The number 666 also has an Old Testament past. The image of Daniel 3 was 60 cubits high, 6 cubits wide and (presumably) 6 cubits deep—666. Also, 666 is the amount of income Solomon received in the year he turned away from the Lord (1 Kings 10:14). To the Hebrew mind-set, the number 666 was a pointer to the apostasy of Solomon, *the son of David.*

So when it comes to the book of Revelation we have to understand that *God meets people where they are.* He gives prophets lessons about the future *in the language—the vocabulary—of the past.* The book of Revelation, like other books of the Bible, comes in the language, culture, and historical setting of the inspired writer.

Ellen White

Finally, from an Adventist perspective, we have the example of Ellen G. White. Many Adventists have assumed God more directly chose her words, that she saw clear pictures of actual events in the future. But even with Ellen White the descriptions of the future came in the language of her past. And what was that? The English language of nineteenth-century America. God met her where she was and worked within that framework.

While Ellen White clearly addressed the future, you will not find a single statement in all of her writings that clearly describes anything that is unique to the twentieth century or beyond. You will look in vain for a description of computers, nuclear war, space travel, the Internet, or any explicit description of the details of World War II in her writings. When she describes events that lie ahead of her times, she does so in vocabulary firmly rooted in her own time and place. For example, when she portrays the wicked forces of the world moving in to attack the saints at the very end of time, what weapons do those wicked carry in their hands? Swords! A description appropriate to the middle of the nineteenth century, but no longer in today's world.

Someone once challenged me on this point. He reminded me of Ellen

White's comments regarding balls of fire falling on New York City at the end. He suggested that it could be a description of nuclear war in our future (more recently some have tried to see the events of September 11, 2001, in the statements). I thought for a moment and then asked if he was familiar with the song, "And the rocket's red glare, the bombs bursting in air, gave proof through the night that our flag was still there." He indicated that he knew the American national anthem.

"Do you know when that song was written?" I asked him.

He thought for a moment. "1814?"

"Right," I said, "Even the language of the fireballs, whatever that will mean when the time comes, is consistent with the language of Ellen White's past." So our knowledge of a more contemporary prophet confirms the evidence collected from our survey of fulfilled prophecies throughout the Bible.

Conclusion

In conclusion, I'd like to share a few practical cautions about prophetic interpretation:

1. I think Christians in general and Adventists in particular tend to be a little too certain that we understand exactly what God plans to do before He does it. Perhaps it arises out of the human temptation to play God, who alone knows the future. But the history of people's interpretations of Revelation ought to be a warning to us. Time and again, interpretations that made perfect sense at one point in time have proved to be dead wrong when the actual fulfillment came. We should not expect point by point correspondence in all details between prophecy and fulfillment. Fulfillments are best recognized when they occur and not before.

2. The primary purpose of prophecy is not to satisfy our curiosity about the future, but to teach us how to live today. God uses a vision of the future to encourage and motivate real people in the actual circumstances of everyday life. Although prophecy is predictive, its goal is to teach us something about God and change the way we live long before the fulfillment comes.

3. We tend to read Revelation as though written to our own time, place, and circumstances. As we do so we bring to our minds associations and concepts that would never have occurred to John or His contempo-

raries. Such readings almost inevitably lead to a distortion of the text and of its original intention. The language of Revelation is that of John's past, not ours.

But if Revelation was written in the vocabulary of another time and place, it raises an important question. How can study of the book be relevant to us in our situation when it speaks to people in another time and place? How can we bridge the gap between their day and ours? And how can we safely find a word from the Lord for today in the writings of those who lived in the distant past? We turn to these questions in the chapters to come.

Principles of Prophetic Interpretation

1. God Is Consistent.
2. God Is Not Predictable.
3. God Is Creative.
4. God Meets People Where They Are.
5. There Is a Spiritualization of the Type.
6. God Uses the Language of the Past to Describe the Future.
7. Prophetic Fulfillments Are Best Recognized After They Occur.

★ Translation and discussion in Hillel Schwartz, *Century's End: A Cultural History of the Fin de Siècle From the 990s Through the 1990s* (New York: Doubleday, 1990). See p. 101.

3

LIVING LESSONS FROM DEAD PROPHETS

I n December of 1974 a man named Donald Yost found two large packages wrapped in paper at the headquarters building of the General Conference of Seventh-day Adventists in Takoma Park, Maryland. The dusty and forgotten packages had lain untouched for more than 50 years. They contained some 2,400 pages of typed, stenographic notes from a lengthy Bible conference held at the General Conference in July and August of 1919. While even historians had nearly forgotten the series of meetings after 50 years, the documents suggested that it had been one of the pivotal moments in Seventh-day Adventist history.

You see, the presence of a living prophet had marked the early decades of the Seventh-day Adventist Church. Adventists believed that the visions and testimonies of Ellen G. White originated from her direct connection with God. From 1844 to 1915 her books, articles, sermons, and private letters provided a constant stream of insight into how God viewed the developing movement. She answered contemporary questions, and her recommendations provided the basis for locating and building denominational institutions. Her work sometimes confirmed the various results of Adventist biblical study and at other times denied them.

The presence of a living prophet provided great challenge, but it also offered great security. Through interaction with the prophet, Adventist leaders could have a strong sense of God's direct guidance in the many difficulties the fledgling movement faced. Theological and political issues could be solved through reference to the prophet's voice. Those fully committed to Ellen White's authority had a sense of certainty that few have in this life.

But in 1915 Ellen White died, stilling the living voice. No longer could the church address the problems of the moment with direct and specific guidance from God. While leaders and members could still consult her writings, one could easily dispute their applicability to specific issues. A church accustomed to the living voice of God in its midst now had to struggle with the writings of a dead prophet, a reality most Christians have always had to live with.

By 1919 the issue of what to do with a dead prophet was becoming an issue of life and death for the young movement. So at the conclusion of the Bible Conference of July 1-21, 1919, the General Conference convened a Bible and History Teacher's Council that continued from July 21 well into the month of August. From July 30 through August 1, 1919, the issue of the dead prophet and her relation to Adventist education and the Bible stood at center stage among the 20 or so delegates, which included many of the leading officers of the General Conference itself. It was a momentous occasion.[1]

A. G. Daniells, president of the General Conference, raised sparks when he described Ellen White's book *The Life of Paul* as "badly put together." "We could never claim inspiration in the whole thought and makeup of the book," he went on. W. W. Prescott then remembered a church controversy over Daniel 8 and reminded the group of Ellen White's letter warning them not to settle such a public controversy over Bible interpretation on the basis of her writings. Daniells responded by telling the group of a personal conversation with Ellen White about an exegetical issue in Daniel 8 (the "daily"), saying that she denied having any revelation on the subject, even though both sides quoted her in support!

The General Conference president and others asserted that Ellen White was no expert in details of history, either. With Daniells in agreement, H. C. Lacey summarized, "In our estimate of the 'spirit of prophecy,' isn't its value to us more in the spiritual light it throws into our own hearts and lives than in the intellectual accuracy in historical and theological matters? Ought we not to take those writings as the voice of the Spirit to our hearts, instead of as the voice of the teacher to our heads? And isn't the final proof of the 'spirit of prophecy' its spiritual value rather than its historical accuracy?"

Things moved on to even more radical ground, at least for some Adventist ears today. Daniells pleaded for common sense in the use of

Ellen White's writings. Vegetarianism is a good principle in general but is not for everyone in every place. Apples may be an excellent food, but Daniells himself got sick when he ate one late in the day! The General Conference president recalled Ellen White serving meat to her husband when he was sick. The whole group swapped stories of how balanced a person the prophet was. They concluded that her writings must be used with caution in daily living and in biblical interpretation.

On the surface of the discussion, all seemed agreed that "verbal inspiration" was not a helpful concept in relation to the writings of Ellen White. They concurred that it required much care and common sense if one was to interpret her writings correctly, especially those regarding the Bible and its interpretation. But after the council a couple of those present began to spread the word that Daniells and other key leaders had abandoned true faith in the prophet. Three years later Daniells found himself ousted from the presidency against his will. The death of a prophet can leave believers with more questions than answers. And the problem of what to do with a dead prophet's writings doesn't diminish with the passage of time.

How do you draw living lessons from the writings of a dead prophet? Ultimately, the answer to that question is the mission of this book. To rightly handle the writings of a dead prophet such as John, you have to begin by taking seriously the time, place, and circumstances in which the biblical author produced the document under study. This is a bottom line for the understanding of any biblical prophecy. But we must also deal with some related questions: How does the Bible text become relevant for today? How can we apply a biblical prophecy to our day, when it was written to somebody else in a different time and place and reflecting a difference of culture, ideas, and language?

Three Approaches to the Bible

There are three different legitimate ways to approach the Bible, and I will call them "exegesis," "biblical theology," and "systematic theology." A chart entitled "Three Ways to Approach Scripture" appears a bit later in this chapter. We will define each procedure in some detail, but first a short definition of each. *Exegesis* has to do with finding out what a writer was attempting to communicate to that original situation, determining his or her intention for the text. It asks the question "What was the writer trying to say?" *Biblical theology,* on the other hand, seeks to determine the big theological picture that lies between the lines and behind what the author wrote. It asks the question "What did the writer believe about . . . God, the end of the world, how to get right with God, etc?" By way of contrast, *systematic theology* tries to determine what truth is in the broadest sense. It asks such questions as "What should I believe?" and "What is God's will for me (for us)?" All three approaches to the Bible are valid, but they each view the Bible in a slightly different way.

Three Ways to Approach Scripture

	Biblical Exegesis	Biblical Theology	Systematic Theology
	"What was the writer trying to say?"	"What did the writer believe?"	"What should I believe? What is truth?"
Time of Reference	first century	first century	twenty-first century
Language	biblical	biblical	philosophical
Result	unchanging	unchanging	changing
Unit of Study	passage	theme	theme
Field of Study	comprehensive	selective	selective
Level of Significance	descriptive	both	normative
Agency Examined	human	both	divine

Biblical Exegesis

For *biblical exegesis* the fundamental question, then, is "What was the Bible writer trying to say?" Since God meets people where they are, the author's original intention is vital for biblical understanding. This places the time of reference for the book of Revelation squarely in the first century. John lived then and under inspiration had something specific to say to specific churches in a particular part of the world. So in describing what John was trying to say, it is helpful to use "biblical categories." In other words, the interpreter should employ John's own language and meanings to explain his book.

You will notice also that exegesis is by definition "unchanging." Our understanding of that text and its manuscript tradition may shift. But what John actually set down to write more than 1,900 years ago has not changed. This means we have an immutable basis for testing various claims to truth outside the Bible. Exegesis is also "passage-oriented," that is, you go verse by verse and text by text. You try to understand line by line what a writer was trying to communicate. In addition, exegesis is also "comprehensive" in that it is a procedure you can perform on any written text. I even do it on student papers, because exegesis is the process of trying to understand the *intention* of the writer at the time when they wrote. The reality is that all of us have some difficulty in communicating. (I struggled a great deal with just how to word this book.) "Comprehensive" means that anything that is written is subject to exegesis.

If you go further down the chart you will see that exegesis is a "descriptive process." It is a method of describing, as best you can, what you think the biblical writer was trying to get across to the reader. Doing so gives you a look at the human side of the Bible. Biblical writers were inspired and received messages from God. But they were also human beings who had friends, family, and the daily issues of life to deal with. They traveled to various places, heard the news, encountered people in business, bought and sold things, ate and drank, and talked to people. Exegesis asks such human-type questions as: "What was the author really intending to say? When John wrote to the churches, what did he want those churches to grasp? What did he understand to be the purpose of the book?"

The process of exegesis is far more relevant than may appear at first sight. By nature we humans protect our favorite ideas by misreading texts that might seem threatening (consciously or unconsciously). Psychologists call this tendency "defense mechanisms." Defense mechanisms go all the way back to Adam and Eve who hid in the bushes from God. One of the best ways to bypass such responses in Bible study is exegesis. You see, a descriptive approach to the Bible does not threaten me. For example, Paul wrote a letter to the Romans. I am not a Roman, so he was not targeting me. My friend Sam Bacchiocchi may be a Roman, but I'm not. And neither Sam nor I live in the first century, so even he is off the hook when it comes to Romans!

The payoff is this: By learning to read the Bible in a descriptive manner, I can be fully honest and open with the text. I can describe what Paul is saying to those first-century Romans. It is no threat to me or my pet ideas. But then an interesting thing happens. Once I have studied a Bible book exegetically, I can never read it the same way again. I will have seen things and thought things that I would never have noticed and envisioned had I taken the text personally. While a descriptive reading of the Bible is not sufficient by itself, it is a marvelous aid toward authenticity in Bible study.

Biblical Theology

As a method, *biblical theology* builds on what the Bible writer was trying to say in order to ask what the biblical author believed. The focus remains on the first century and on the use of biblical categories. Biblical theology is also unchanging. Why is that? Well, I don't think John or Paul have had a new thought in the past 2,000 years! Since they are dead, they are no longer thinking, writing, or theologizing. So what John or Paul believed is something unique to the first century. We have in their writings a solid, unchanging source of information about God.

Up to this point, biblical exegesis and biblical theology are identical in basic approach. But differences do exist between them. When doing biblical theology, instead of studying passages, you explore themes and ideas. You ask such questions as: "What did John believe about the end of the world?" The minute you deal in themes, you also become selective. If you were to ask, "What was John's view on salvation?" for example, you might look at some passages in Revelation but not at others. You wouldn't examine every part of the book equally because your theme is "salvation," and texts that have nothing to do with salvation would not be of interest to you at that point. If you were to ask the question "What was Jeremiah's view on health?" you would probably find very little on that subject in the book of Jeremiah, because it doesn't address that theme. So thematic questions about what a writer believed are very selective. You pick only the material that addresses your question.

Is biblical theology a descriptive process? Yes and no. On the one hand, biblical theology is descriptive, because you are trying to portray what John and Paul believed. But it is also normative, because what John or Paul believed as an inspired prophet is a rule for your life whenever your circumstances are similar to those being addressed. In other words, when faced with similar situations, what was true then is equally true now.

Suppose the prophet were to say something about health or a certain lifestyle. Such a principle would probably not change as long as our bodies are fairly similar to the way they were back then. Circumstances alter cases, but where the circumstances are analogous, the principles have the same authority now as they did in the prophet's lifetime.

Is biblical theology human or divine? Again the answer needs to be yes and no. In part, it's a human process because Paul and John were human beings. But through inspiration those human beings also spoke for God (1 Peter 1:18).

Systematic Theology

In *systematic theology,* by way of contrast, everything seems to change. When you ask what you should believe, what God's will is for you, you move the point of focus from the first to the twenty-first century. Now, instead of the biblical categories of exegesis, you're asking your questions in your own language. The language of systematic theology is not "biblical," but rather "philosophical." What do I mean by that? Every person has a philosophy—some people know it and some don't. But philosophy is more than simply a view about the world. It's what you think about how things are put together, where we came from, where we're going, why we're here, etc. Everyone has a certain philosophy of life. When you ask philosophical questions, you're asking the personal questions that burn in your heart.

Philosophical questions by definition include issues that John never heard of or that the Bible never addresses. An example: "Should a Christian smoke?" Nowhere does the Bible deal with the subject of tobacco. People in the Old World didn't discover tobacco until about the sixteenth century. So we know that the Bible doesn't directly address the issue of smoking.

Can you, therefore, address the question of smoking from the Bible alone? I would suggest that you can't. Ultimately, the reason that many Christians reject smoking is not a biblical reason but a scientific one. Yes, one can talk about the biblical principle that God wants us to be stewards of our bodies, which He so lovingly made. Scientifically, however, Christians have come to realize that tobacco products damage the human body. Moving beyond science, many people experience the harmful effects of smoking firsthand. They wheeze, cough, annoy others, and experience smoking-related health problems. So where smoking is concerned, the evidence seems clear even though the Bible doesn't address the issue directly.

Systematic theology, then, is not always directly dependent on the Bible for its answers. When you ask what God's will is for you, you are not limited to what the Bible says. The possibilities for theological study are almost endless. Can you find God's will through the study of psychology? Yes. Why? Because the Bible says that we are all created in the image of God. If that is true, then as you study the mind, you can learn something about the God that created it. Sociology can teach us how groups of human beings created in the image of God relate to one another. History can show us the successes and failures of those who have, or have not, tried to carry out God's will. History, sociology, science, spiritual gifts, experience, the writings of Ellen White—all are ways to find out God's will for us. Systematic theology is not limited to the Bible. It asks open-ended questions: "What is truth? What is God's will for me? What is God's will for all of us?"

Let me illustrate the difference between systematic theology and the biblical approaches. A student once came to me and wanted to do a dissertation on the subject of "Sanctification in the Book of Revelation." I told him he couldn't do that.

"What do you mean that I can't do that?" he protested.

"You're wanting to do biblical theology, to study what John believed about sanctification," I explained. "There's only one small problem—John never used the word. You would have to go outside Revelation, or even the Bible, to deal with the question. So it would be like mixing apples and oranges. If you want to know what John believed about character growth, Christian life and Christian development, you're not going to find it in the word 'sanctification.'"

I suggested instead that he could do a dissertation on "good works" in the book of Revelation. Revelation *does* use the word "works." John *is* interested in how people behave after they become Christians, but he doesn't employ the word "sanctification" to describe it. I suggested to this student that if he wanted to do a dissertation on the book of Revelation, he should use the actual words of John with the meanings that he intended. To do otherwise would lead to an endless and confusing result.

When studying the Bible, we should not to mix our own philosophical use of language with that of the Bible. If we ask the question "What is the biblical view of sanctification?" we need to let the biblical writers define the terms and not assume that the word meant the same thing to them that it does to us. Luther employed the word "sanctification" in a way that Paul didn't. When we use Luther's definitions to study Paul, we distort Paul. And when we apply our contemporary definitions while studying Revelation, we can warp the meaning of the biblical book. John did not write it in the twenty-first century, but in A.D. 95. It is to that time and place that we need to go if we are to rightly understand the author's intention. And since Jesus met John where he was, we will also discern His intention for us in that original situation.

Notice on the previous chart that the time of reference for systematic theology is the twenty-first century, its terminology is philosophical, and the status of its results is constantly changing. Why is systematic theology changeable by definition? Because the questions we ask constantly keep shifting. We are asking new questions not raised in past centuries and that the Bible writers never addressed, such as: "Should women be ordained? Should Christians smoke? What role should television and the Internet play in a Christian's life?"

As the questions alter, new answers must develop to meet them. So we could say that *circumstances alter cases*. As circumstances change, the will of God sometimes adjusts to help us deal with differing situations. This is not to say that God is changing His mind in the ultimate sense, but that He meets people where they are. We have seen that principle again and again in Scripture. As circumstances and questions shift, God is able to accommodate Himself in such a way as to communicate in the living language of the people.

Notice that systematic theology, like biblical theology, is thematic and selective. As we ask our philosophical questions, we are setting a theme and in the process automatically choosing our sources. When it comes to smoking, as we have seen, we find a basic principle in the biblical doctrine of taking care of our bodies, but we will discover how to apply that principle in detail only through scientific study. If somebody came up with a cigarette that was good for us, there is no biblical reason not to smoke *that* type of cigarette. It is for scientific reasons alone that we accept the chewing of spinach and reject the chewing of tobacco.

On the bottom of the chart you'll notice the words "normative" and "divine." Systematic theology has to do with normative truths. The word normative means "a rule for life"—how people ought to live. Examples of normative questions are: "Should a Christian smoke?" "What is God's plan for my life?" and "Is premarital sex appropriate for a Christian?" When we get a clear answer from God (regardless of the source) to any of these questions, it becomes a law for our being. "Normative" has to do with the way we are expected to live.

Systematic theology, in the way I am defining it, is also divine in that it assumes that there is a God and that He has an opinion on the particular subject. We are seeking to understand how He wants us to live. In this sense systematic theology is very personal and very practical. It can play a similar role for the church at large, "What is truth?" "What is God's will or plan for us?"

From Then to Now

The chart we began with summarizes three ways of approaching Scripture. Christians sometimes try to mix and match them. A church may claim, for example, that it follows the Bible and the Bible only. But if that church teaches that Christians shouldn't smoke, is it 100 percent accurate to say it follows the Bible and the Bible only? Isn't it also true that science has played a role in coming to that decision? As we raise questions on whether or not to ordain women, for example, are we not arguing also from psychology, sociology, history, and experience, as well as from the evidence of biblical passages?

Although Adventists try to bring all beliefs to the test of Scripture, we should not think of the 27 fundamental beliefs of the Seventh-day Adventist Church as biblical theology. We can more accurately understand them as systematic theology. They express what the church as a whole thinks God wants people to believe and practice in today's world. The kinds of issues addressed in the fundamentals go far beyond those touched upon in the Bible. Perhaps 30 per cent of the Adventist fundamentals need support from science, history, experience, the writings of Ellen White, and other sources outside the Bible. Other fundamentals are based on texts as understood in terms of a wider contemporary meaning, not just the exegetical significance of that text. And there is nothing wrong with that. We don't want to limit ourselves just to exegetical understandings. Scripture needs to be applied in creative ways to the issues of today's world.

What about the writings of Ellen White? Are we to understand them as exegesis, biblical theology, or systematic theology? Many have assumed that Ellen White's use of Scripture was exegetical. They are often eager to limit exegesis of biblical texts to the constraints of her offhand comments about them. But careful analysis over time has led the White Estate to conclude that Ellen White rarely attempted to do exegesis along the lines we have discussed in this chapter.[2] Less then 1 percent of the time does she attempt to answer the question: "What was the biblical writer trying to say?" I believe that a high percentage of her exegetical statements occur in the books *Thoughts From the Mount of Blessing, Christ's Object Lessons,* and *The Acts of the Apostles.* Exegetical statements are extremely rare in the *Testimonies* and most of her other writings.

Like most biblical prophets, she was relatively uninterested in the original meaning of the biblical texts she used. She was more concerned to draw out the large principles and perspectives from the insights gained in her direct connection to God. Thus she did not need to do exegesis of the Bible to attain those insights. I suspect that she drew most of her exegetical statements not from her visionary insights, but from books on the same topic that she read and decided to incorporate into her own work (that is certainly true of *The Acts of the Apostles*). We will address these issues in more detail shortly.

What about the proof-text method so popular in Bible studies and evangelistic presentations? Is it exegesis, biblical theology, or systematic theology? At its best, I like to think of it as biblical theology. It is the attempt to draw together all the biblical references on a particular subject with the purpose of determining what the overall teaching of the Bible on that subject is. Done properly, the proof-text method should use biblical citations in ways that do not contradict their exegetical meaning, but by comparing passage with passage the method will tend to draw out a larger picture than the individual authors of the Bible may have understood.

As Adventists approach the book of Revelation, they have a natural tendency to ask questions of the book that its author never attempted to answer. If we try to find in it the outcome of the Israeli-Palestinian conflict or whether a certain American president will be the one who precipitates the final crisis of earth's history, we will eventual discover that the Bible doesn't address the question. If the Bible doesn't deal with the issue, our attempt to get that kind of information out of Revelation will only distort the book's intent.

When approaching Revelation, therefore, I believe it is critical to begin with the method of exegesis: "What was John trying to say when he wrote the book of Revelation?" We must discover the significance that his words had in their time and place. And we need to try to understand the God who meets people where they are. After we've finished the basic groundwork, we can move on to explore the bigger theological picture of Revelation, including the meaning it should have for us today.

Practical Implications

Perhaps you are wondering why we have to do exegesis when Paul and Ellen White didn't have to. I think there is a very good reason. You and I are in a very different situation from either of them. You see, prophets do not need to do exegesis. It's a matter of authority. Let me explain.

The Source of Authority

Authority, in the ultimate sense, resides in God and Him alone. Anyone else carries spiritual authority only to the extent that they speak for God. For example, suppose I said to you, "Last night I had a dream, and in that dream God told me, 'You ought to sell everything you've got and move to Africa.'" Would you do it? That depends, I suppose, on whether or not you believe God actually gave me that dream!

Now, if you believe that I am a prophet (and I'm not) and that my dream came directly from Him (remember, this is only hypothetical), you might take it quite seriously, wouldn't you? You might even start inquiring about airfares and job opportunities in Africa. But if you didn't believe that I spoke for God or that He sent me that dream, it should have absolutely no authority in your thinking, right?

The prophet's authority lies in the fact that he or she has a direct line to God! The genuine prophet receives revelations from God, often in visions and dreams, so when he or she gives messages to people, it is as if they came directly from God Himself. If God directly tells a person to sell everything and move to Africa, the individual had better do it. That message has "normative" authority.

It is different with you and me. We have no direct line with God the way a prophet does. That is why exegesis is so important. As nonprophets we need to do exegesis because the only absolutely reliable window we have to the mind of God is to rightly understand His Word. Without direct access to God or to a living prophet, we must base our understanding of truth on sound, careful examination of the words of inspiration.

Paul didn't have to do exegesis of the Old Testament in order to know the truth about God. The basis of the apostle's authority was not the soundness of his study, but the genuineness of his direct access to God. Sometimes Paul applies the writings of the Old Testament prophets in ways they wouldn't have recognized or to circumstances that the earlier prophet wouldn't have foreseen. But that is all right as long as he is functioning under God's direction. God helped Paul to utilize the writings of dead prophets to create a living message for his time and place. The authority that comes through in Paul's letters is that of God. But I do not have the kind of authority that he had. He was inspired. His conclusions carry their own authority. But *my conclusions have authority only as they accurately reflect the biblical content.*

If careful exegesis is important in the gospels or the letters of Paul, how much more is it important to the study of Revelation, a book that evokes as many opinions as there are interpreters of it. So in the previous chapter we took a careful look at the big picture of the Bible. From that we've drawn some basic principles upon which to base our study of Revelation. Careful biblical work is necessary because I have no authority from God to write a book about Revelation unless I rightly handle the texts that He has already given. I carry authority only to the extent that I am accurately reflecting what is actually there in the biblical text.

Dead Prophets

What you and I face is a problem faced by most generations: the problem of the dead prophet. As indicated in the title of this chapter, we are interested in "Living Lessons." But the place where we must go to find those living lessons is to the writings of dead prophets. God gave His revelations in the context of another time, another place, and other circumstances. Yet we go there to hear a word from the Lord for us—for our time and our place.

How then do we find living lessons in the dead prophets without reading into the Bible our own prejudices and pet ideas? Through a careful application of all three approaches suggested above. 1. If we want a living lesson that has the authority of God behind it, we must be prepared to understand first what John's intention was and what God's intention was in working through him. 2. The next step is to move beyond the text to understand John's basic philosophy of life, the bigger picture of his theology that he applied in that text. 3. Finally we need to ask the questions of today. We need to find out how the great principles reflected in the text apply to the real issues of living in the contemporary world.

But as important as exegesis is, we can't stop there. God's intention for Scripture is not limited to the original human author's purpose but is expressed through it. Systematic theology compares scripture with scripture and sees things that the original writer never had in mind. Later history and later revelations may expose extended meanings present in God's intention but not the human author's.

But how do we know that such an extended meaning of the text is valid and has the authority of God behind it? Only if that *extended meaning is a natural expansion of the plain meaning of the original text.* We can only trust the extended meaning when we know the original meaning and the original intention of the passage. Systematic theology can mislead us unless it is grounded in careful exegesis of the biblical text.

Do we always have to do exegesis when reading the Bible? No. Many times during a devotional experience God will touch one's heart with a sense of what is right. For personal use in our own lives, God can often bypass the exegetical meaning of the text to teach us something. But exegesis is not a devotional approach. It has to do with Christians searching for truth as a body. If a group of people seeks a common understanding of the Bible, it is important that they are all reading the same text! If everybody in the group brings their own ideas, feelings, and impressions to a passage and then insists that those impressions are the word of God, they can never have unity of understanding.

Antioch and Alexandria

How do we safely find living lessons in the writings of dead prophets? Historically, Christians have employed two ways of trying to make the text of the Bible relevant for today. Those two approaches are sometimes associated with two ancient cities—Antioch and Alexandria. Each became identified with a method of reading the Bible. The approach of Alexandria is called "allegory." The method of Antioch was close to what we have called exegesis.

Allegory seems to have started with Plato, a philosopher who lived about four centuries before the time of Jesus. According to Homer (800 B.C.), whose writings were the "Bible" of the ancient Greeks, the gods of the Greeks were just like human beings in character, but had absolute power. The idea left Plato unimpressed, however. *God is not like that,* he thought. *The true God is much greater than that.* Plato saw a clearer picture of God than most Greeks had, but his own teacher, Socrates, had been martyred for teaching such ideas. Not eager to experience a similar fate, Plato developed the allegorical approach to Homer's writings. Through allegory he was able to reshape the teachings of Homer in such a way that the Greek writer seemed to be presenting what Plato was trying to teach. So allegory saved Plato's life by reducing the tension between his views and the sacred writings of the ancient Greeks.

People have frequently applied allegory to the Bible as well, beginning with the work of Philo and Origen in the ancient world. A classic example of allegory is Origen's interpretation of the parable of the good Samaritan. Origen did not ask how the story functioned in Jesus' original purpose. Instead, for Origen, the story became a parable teaching his own third-century theology. The victim in the story is Adam; Jerusalem represents heaven; and Jericho, the world. The traveler is Adam going from heaven to the world. The robbers are Satan and his angels. The priest represents the law; the Levite, the prophets; and the Samaritan, Christ. The donkey is Christ's body who carries the fallen Adam. The inn represents the church and the two coins paid by the Samaritan are the Father and the Son. His promise to come back and pay the bills in the future represents Jesus promise to return—the Second Coming.

Origen of Alexandria certainly added a fresh dimension to the story. No doubt his interpretation made it more interesting to his audience. But does it have anything to do with the original meaning of that parable? Hardly. Origen has allegorized the story by bringing in ideas and concepts from his time. By reading into the story ideas from his own standpoint in time, he has used the story to do something entirely different than what Jesus intended. This is, in fact, the natural way humans approach the Bible. Most of us read the biblical text in light of our own needs, ideas, and questions.

The ancient city of Antioch, on the other hand, had an exegetical approach to Scripture, insisting that the biblical text itself must govern the content of what an interpreter sees in it. We must take the original setting into account. Only after we understand the original setting should we make any application to our own time and place. So the basic concepts of exegesis have had almost as long a history as allegory.

Allegory was triumphant during the Middle Ages. The medieval church used allegory to confirm its own teachings from the Bible, no matter how foreign to the gospel they might be. This led people far from Scripture and from the will of God. With the coming of the Protestant Reformation, however, the spirit of Antiochean exegesis revived. The Bible was once again the final word in the search for truth. The Reformation promoted a return to the Bible and the meanings inherent in it.

Alexandria is far from dead, however, even in Protestant churches. Allegory is very intriguing, so preachers use it to apply the Bible to the needs, concerns, and issues of their churches. In so doing, they unconsciously impose these needs and concerns on the original context of the Bible. Usually it is not something done consciously. In fact, one could argue that allegory is the "natural" way to read the Bible. It's not necessarily dangerous if the interpreter's theology is sound. But the conclusions of allegory say more about the interpreter's theology than the meaning of the biblical text. If we want to understand a complex book such as Revelation, we need to examine carefully how we are reading it.

In the last half of this book I lay out in considerable detail what it means to do exegesis on the book of Revelation. I have drawn the method from the evidence in the text itself. It is the method of Antioch, allowing the text itself to govern what we see in it. In the future I plan to apply this approach consistently to all 22 chapters of Revelation.

In the next chapter I will examine some guidelines and safeguards to pastors and laypeople who may not have some of the scholarly tools but who would like to study and teach the book of Revelation in an exegetical way. The guidelines I present offer a practical tour through the city of Antioch. Through these tools people living everyday lives can overcome the natural tendency to allegorize the Bible. They can gain a genuine understanding of the biblical text that will help them grow into the knowledge of God.

---

[1] In my summary of the council discussions I am particularly indebted to the transcripts and introduction found in *Spectrum* 10, no. 1 (1979): 23-57.

[2] Cf. the comments by Robert Olson in *Ministry,* December 1990, p. 17.

4

SAFEGUARDS FOR BIBLICAL STUDY

We all face a major problem when we open the Bible: self-deception. One Scripture deals directly with this danger: "The heart is deceitful above all things and beyond cure. Who can understand it?" (Jer. 17:9, NIV). The problem described here is self-deception. Your heart is deceitful. My heart is deceitful. In fact, our hearts are so devious that we don't even realize how much we deceive ourselves. This has major implications for the way we approach the Bible. As I noted above, the Alexandrian approach is the "natural" way to read the Bible. It is easy for us to project our own ideas, concepts, and needs into Scripture and turn the Bible into a book that reads just the way we believe.

When I'm doing systematic theology—asking questions about what is truth for me—my defense mechanisms (remember them?) get involved. Human beings naturally—even unconsciously—tend to avoid ideas and situations that would be painful to them. So whenever we come face-to-face with the Bible, knowing that we are looking for truth, the natural defense mechanisms of sin get in the way. If we see something in the Bible that will call us wrong—call us sinners—we like to avoid that as much as possible. So it is natural to read the Bible in such a way as to escape having to learn what we don't want to know.

But there is a way out of this dilemma. The best remedy for self-deception is exegesis. Exegesis helps us bypass the defense mechanisms that cause us to misread the Bible. I've developed a definition of exegesis that is kind of fun. It goes like this: "Exegesis is the art of learning how to read the Bible in such a way as to leave open the possibility that you might learn something." Often we study the Bible but don't absorb anything because we don't want to discover that what we are doing is wrong and that we may have to change. So, as Jeremiah 17:9 points out, it is natural for us to deceive ourselves—even as we are studying the Bible.

But exegesis can help us deal with self-deception because it invites a descriptive approach to the Bible. A descriptive approach means that the internal pressure to distort the Bible's meaning gets turned off. If I am describing what John is saying to the churches of Asia Minor in the first century, I don't have to feel any duress, because I'm not a member of a congregation in Asia Minor and I don't live in the first century. So exegesis allows us to face the reality of God's Word. I can describe what John was saying to them without it necessarily affecting me. By removing the internal pressure, I can be more honest with the text than I would otherwise be.

But here's the best part. Once we have exegeted a biblical text, we can never read it the same way again. We cannot avoid the deeper implications of that passage as we might have been able to before. Exegesis opens the way for the Bible to touch our hearts with just what we need to know and understand.

The Role of the Original Languages

The best safeguard against self-deception is an exegesis based on the original languages, the Greek and the Hebrew. Genuine descriptive exegesis is more difficult for me in English (my native language), because English is filled with associations to my own, personal past. As a child I heard English being used in my home. Every word in that language came to me in the context of a certain time, place, and circumstance. So for me, every word of the Bible triggers associations with my own personal history. It evokes the events and situations in which I encountered those words and the meanings those words had in those contexts. As a result it's almost impossible not to project my own ideas into the Bible when I read it in English. Projecting one's self into the Bible is perfectly natural until one becomes conscious of the need to learn a better way of reading Scripture.

Learning to read the New Testament in the Greek, however, allows one to break the bonds of the past and experience the text as the author meant it to be perceived when it was first written. Biblical Greek is taught in terms of its original background. Students of biblical Greek use lexicons and dictionaries to unpack words in the context of the first-century world. To learn the Greek of the New Testament is to break away from the familiar associations that blind interpreters to the deeper connections of the text. When interpreters develop a reading knowledge of the Greek New Testament, connections between words, phrases, and texts start popping up that they would not have seen in translation.

Some people raise the question "Well, if that's the case, wouldn't modern Greeks have a special advantage over us in reading the book of Revelation?" No, actually they would be at some disadvantage. Greeks today learn their language the same way you and I acquire English or whatever your native language is. For Greeks it is a natural tendency to see modern meanings in the ancient language of the Greek New Testament.

I realize, however, that most people reading this book will never have the opportunity to learn Greek or to become specialists in the ancient time, place, and circumstances of the book of Revelation. Still, is it possible to do serious, honest exegesis? I believe it is. I'd like to suggest six study safeguards that will help anyone interpret the biblical text while avoiding the kind of bizarre misreadings that come so naturally to the human condition. These six principles provide interpreters with the kind of biblical balance necessary to deal with a difficult book such as Revelation.

1. Begin With Authentic Prayer and Self-distrust

When you open the Bible, it is important to do so with much prayer and self-distrust. If human hearts are exceedingly wicked and deceptive, then the greatest barrier to scriptural understanding is the lack of a teachable spirit. Without a teachable spirit, it doesn't matter how much Greek you know or how many Ph.D.s you accumulate. Your learning will not open the Word to you. True knowledge of God does not come from merely intellectual pursuit or academic study. It arises from a willingness to receive the truth no matter what the cost.

Texts that underline this principle are:

"The man without the Spirit does not accept the things that come from the Spirit of God, for they are foolishness to him, and he cannot understand them, because they are spiritually discerned" (1 Cor. 2:14, NIV).

"They perish because they refused to love the truth and so be saved" (2 Thess. 2:10, NIV).

"If any of you lacks wisdom, he should ask God, who gives generously to all without finding fault, and it will be given to him" (James 1:5, NIV).

Knowledge of God comes from a willingness to receive the truth from God no matter what. But it can cost you your life, your family, your friends, and your reputation. So how badly do you really want to know God? If you want the truth no matter the price, you will receive it. God is willing for you to find the truth if you are willing to be taught.

So I'd like to suggest that you begin your study of the book of Revelation with what I call authentic prayer. That means prayer for a teachable spirit. Prayer that God will open your heart, bypass your defense mechanisms, and teach you what you need to know. Authentic prayer goes something like this: "Lord, I want the truth about the book of Revelation no matter what it demands of me personally." That's a hard prayer to offer. But that kind of prayer will open the way to fresh insight into the Word.

2. Use a Variety of Translations

If you are not familiar with the Greek and Hebrew, an excellent alternative is to consult a variety of translations. Every translation has its limitations and weaknesses and to some degree reflects the biases of the translator(s). So the safest course of action for a Christian who doesn't know the original languages is to compare several translations against each other.

Let's suppose you are checking a particular text against five different translations. If all five agree, the underlying Greek text must be reasonably clear. That is the kind of text upon which you can base your faith with confidence. On the other hand, if all five translations go in different directions, it signals that the original language is ambiguous in some way. You will want to be cautious about insisting that any particular translation of the text reflects the original. And you will be reluctant to base your belief system on an unclear text.

But what if four translations say roughly the same thing, but the fifth one is way off in another county? That is usually a clue toward figuring out the tendency of that particular translation. Every translation has some bias or another, and through careful comparison you can develop a sense for it. The authority that you as an interpreter give to any particular translation of a text will depend on the level of certainty that it is accurately based on the original. Looking at a variety of translations can give anyone a clearer picture of the original text.

Using a variety of translations, of course, helps us overcome pet readings of the text. We all have favorite passages that mean certain things to us. When we pick up a new translation, it is fun to go right to those particular ones to see how that version has rendered it. We are often disappointed when we do this. The translator just didn't see what we do. But honesty will compel us to acknowledge that we often twist the actual meaning of a verse to maintain a favorite or pet reading. Because we prefer a certain reading of the text, we cannot see its real significance in its original context. Being open to a variety of translations, however, enables us to become more honest with the passage.

3. Favor the Clear Texts

If you want to let the Scriptures speak for themselves, spend the majority of your time in the sections of Scripture that are reasonably clear. The Bible contains much that Christians agree upon. Many parts are extremely easy to understand, and others are extremely difficult. A great safeguard to your study of Scripture is to spend the majority of your time in the unambiguous sections. The clear texts of Scripture establish the reader in the common ground of the Bible and the great verities of its message, safeguarding the interpreter against an inappropriate use of texts that are more cryptic.

Adventists in particular seem to gravitate to the ambiguous texts of the Bible—passages difficult to understand because they can point in more than one direction. People who misuse the Bible tend to work with vague texts, treat them as if they were clear, and then base their theology on their particular reading. When people dwell on the difficult texts of Scripture, they usually end up having to distort noncontroversial texts of Scripture because the message of the clear texts contradicts the theology they have developed from the obscure ones. That is one reason for the many bizarre readings of Revelation. The book attracts people who love to play with the edges of Scripture, people who have an unhealthy need to find something new, fresh, and exciting to share with others.

If you spend the most of your study time in passages such as Daniel 11, the seals, and the trumpets, however, you will probably go crazy, spiritually if not psychologically. Such passages are extremely difficult, and it's easy to distort them and make them carry a weight they were never meant to bear. But if you devote the majority of your time to the clear texts of the Bible, they will safeguard you against making an inappropriate use of the seals and trumpets or anything else. Immersion in the unambiguous parts of the Bible keeps you from applying less-clear texts in ways that contradict the central teachings of the Bible.

4. Favor General Reading

A fourth, and most vital, principle is to compare the results of your Bible study with much general reading of Scripture so that the obsession with detail doesn't lead you away from the central thrust of the Bible. People often approach the Bible in a fragmented way. They study a verse at a time and then compare that verse with all kinds of other texts found in a concordance. In a way the concordance becomes their real Bible. They take a word, look at snippets from 300-400 texts, and pick out those that seem to declare what they want the Bible to teach. This method can even tempt preachers.

Sometimes they will come to the night before a sermon and realize at 10:00 or 11:00 p.m. that they are not ready for the sermon that they need to present the next day. So they bid the family good night and retire to the study. First they think about the congregation and the kind of message that would encourage and strengthen it. By 12:30 a.m. an outline begins to form. Before long the message is looking pretty good. But before such preachers head for bed they reach for a concordance. For what purpose? To find a few Bible texts that seem to support their theme.

What are they doing? Cloaking their own ideas in the trappings of Scripture. The sermon did not develop out of the Bible but arose from their reflection on a real-life situation. By sprinkling the sermon with a variety of texts drawn from a concordance, they attempt to undergird their ideas with the apparent authority of the Bible. The best safeguard against such unintentional misuse of Scripture is extensive general reading of the Bible. Broad immersion in the Bible sensitizes you to the literary strategies of the biblical authors. Use of a concordance, on the other hand, puts you in charge of the process, instead of the biblical writer.

Employing a concordance and the comparison of scripture with scripture has its place. As we work our way through the book of Revelation, we will do a lot of it. Sometimes we will compare Revelation with the Old Testament, sometimes with other parts of the New, and occasionally with sources outside the Bible. All of this will help us understand what John's original intention for Revelation was. But when you spend all of your time matching one passage with another you can lose the forest for the trees. General reading of the Bible, on the other hand, makes one sensitive to the larger context of Scripture.

For general reading I recommend a modern translation that is easy to follow. While the King James Version, for example, is very helpful for deep study, I have great difficulty keeping up with the flow of the story or thought from one chapter to the next. General reading helps you to look at the big picture and put isolated texts together with their contexts so that the meaning can become clear. With a concordance, on the other hand, we tend to isolate verses from their contexts. Concordance study, without the control of broad reading, is like cutting 50 texts out of the Bible, tossing them like a salad in a bowl, and finally pulling them out one by one and announcing, "This is the Word of the Lord."

The process is all the more dangerous when done on a computer. Computers have wonderful Bible programs in which you can enter a word or two and discover all the texts that have that word or combination of words. I have such a program myself and find it extremely useful. But Bible programs make it so easy to play with the ideas of the Bible that you may never actually read the Bible itself. The meanings that you draw from computer texts may have nothing to do with the biblical author's original intention.

General reading of the Bible allows the interpreter to get the "big picture" view of Scripture. It safeguards the reader against bizarre interpretations of its isolated parts. Also, such general reading helps bring you into a teachable spirit and enables you to see the text as God and the biblical author intended it to be read. Hence the recommendation, "Spend the majority of your time reading the Bible instead of studying it."

5. Give Attention to Criticism of Peers

A vital principle for the study of Revelation is to give careful attention to the counsel and criticism of peers. A peer is anyone who has given the text the same kind of careful attention you have. The most valuable of peers, in fact, is the person who disagrees with you or is particularly gifted or experienced with the tools of exegesis. As I mentioned before, one of the biggest problems in biblical understanding is that each of us have a natural bent to self-deception (Jer. 17:9). That self-deception is so deep that sometimes—even if you are praying, using a variety of translations, and focusing on the clear texts and broad reading—you can still misread the Bible on your own. So the best antidote to such self-deception is to constantly subject one's own understandings to the evaluation of others who are making equally rigorous efforts to understand those same texts.

It reminds me of Alcoholics Anonymous and the process called "intervention." When it comes to alcohol, alcoholics are usually the last person to know that they have a problem. Professionals, therefore, recommend the process of intervention in which family, friends, acquaintances, and authority figures gather and say, "Yes, you are an alcoholic, and I saw you do this or that."

As they confront the alcoholic time and time again with the facts, it becomes more likely that he or she will eventually recognize that they do have a problem and will seek help. I'd like to suggest that intervention is often necessary with exegesis of the Bible as well. We require the critiques of others who say, "I've looked at this text carefully, and I just don't see what you are seeing. To me the text says something totally different."

It may be painful to listen to that kind of criticism. But it is the only way to avoid what I call the Saddam Hussein syndrome. You see, none of Saddam Hussein's advisors ever disagreed with him, because everyone who did was soon dead. As a result, he usually got very bad advice. I can imagine him asking his advisors before both Gulf Wars, "What do you think? Can we beat the coalition gathering against us?" No doubt the unanimous answer was "If you are in charge, we can't lose." Bad advice! But that is what you get when you don't listen to people who disagree with you.

You see, I don't learn much from people who agree with me, because we already view things the same way. It is people who disagree with me, who see the text differently than I do, who can teach me something about the passage. When I am confronted with someone very different from me—someone of another culture or even another religion—I find myself facing realities in the text that I would never have seen on my own. I may not end up agreeing with Roman Catholic conclusions about Revelation,

86

but a Roman Catholic will notice things in the text that I would miss (and vice versa). Thus the insights of others deepens my own knowledge of God's Word.

People I disagree with vigorously will see things in the text that I would never notice because of my blind spots and my defense mechanisms. The other person may be just as messed up as I am, but if that individual has a different set of defense mechanisms and blind spots than I do, he or she will still observe things in the text that I would miss and I will see things that they will overlook. We can see much more clearly together than separately. Even in the study of the Bible we need to listen to others, particularly people who have also explored Scripture carefully and have come to different conclusions than we have.

6. Use Ellen White Appropriately

Seventh-day Adventists need to address one further issue. Ellen G. White's comments on the book of Revelation stimulate much productive insight, but we can use her writings in a way that obscures the meaning of the biblical text and makes it serve the agenda of the interpreter.[1] Offhand comments in various contexts can get universalized or applied in ways that run counter to the implications of the biblical text itself. Such use is really abuse and results in diminishing her authority rather than enhancing it.

Inspiration is truly handled with respect when we permit the intention of an inspired writer to emerge from the text in its original context (exegesis). As we noted in the previous chapter, messages from living prophets can easily be clarified upon request. But once the prophet has passed from the scene, we are on safest ground when we allow the intent of each inspired text to emerge by means of careful exegesis.[2]

The role of inspiration is particularly problematic with regard to Ellen White's use of Scripture. An interpreter with a strong preconceived idea can easily utilize her scriptural quotations in such a way as to overthrow the plain meaning of the text in its biblical context.[3] Inferences drawn from the text of Revelation are at times creatively combined with deductions drawn from the Spirit of Prophecy to produce a result that cannot be plainly demonstrated from either source. Though usually well-intentioned, it diverts the people of God from careful attention to the plain meaning of the text, and thus encourages careless methods of interpretation that can damage the cause of God. With the goal of safeguarding her inspired in-tention, six tentative guidelines for the use of Ellen White in the study of Revelation follow.

1. Quotation or Echo?

First, it is important to determine whether Ellen White was intending to cite a particular biblical text or was merely "echoing" it. If she quotes the passage and gives a reference, the matter is fairly clear. But often she uses biblical words or phrases in isolation and without apparent reference to their original context. In such cases it isn't immediately clear if she was aware that she was using biblical language or if that vocabulary just flowed naturally from her past experience with the Bible.

The procedure for determining allusions that we explain in chapter 7 will be helpful in ascertaining her intention as well. If we conclude that she is not quoting a Bible text, but merely echoing its language, we should not assume that she is expressing a judgment on the biblical writer's intention for that particular passage. She may be drawing a valid spiritual lesson when she echoes Scripture, but it is not necessarily the same one the biblical writer was trying to impress upon readers.

2. Exegetical, Theological, or Homiletical?

Second, where Ellen White clearly refers the reader to a scriptural pas-sage, we should ask how she is using the passage. Is she using it exegetically—making a statement about the original meaning of the passage in the author's context? Is she using it theologically—discussing the implication that passage has for a larger theology based on Scripture as a whole and focusing particu-larly on God's will for her readers? Or is she using it homiletically—playing with the power of the biblical language in a preaching situation?[4]

To interpret a homiletical use as though it were an exegetical state-ment will distort not only her intention but the meaning of the biblical statement as well. While more study needs to be done on this question, it is my opinion that Ellen White rarely uses Scripture exegetically (i.e., being primarily concerned with the biblical writer's intent).[5] As was the case with the classical prophets of the Old Testament, her main concern was to speak to her contemporary situation. She normally uses Scripture theologically and homiletically rather than exegetically.

To say this is not to limit Ellen White's authority. We should always take her intention in a given statement with utmost seriousness. At the same time we must be careful not to limit the authority of the biblical writer. Never should we deny a biblical writer's intention on the basis of a homiletical usage of a Bible passage. What I am pleading for here is that we learn to respect Ellen White's own intention in her use of biblical material. Since she often employs Scripture in other than exegetical ways, we must examine with great care statements quoting Revelation before we dogmatically apply them in the exegesis of the biblical book.[6]

3. Published or Unpublished?

Third, Ellen White herself makes a distinction between her published writings and other material.[7] We can best understand her theological intention in the writings that she most carefully wrote and edited. Offhand comments, in letters or stenographically reproduced from sermons, may not reflect her settled opinion on timeless issues. Compilations of her writings by others need to be used even more cautiously, since the selection and ordering of material can, in itself, make a theological statement. If something appears only in letters and manuscripts—particularly if it occurs only once—the interpreter needs to demonstrate that it is a true reflection of her considered and consistent intent.

4. Central or Peripheral?

Fourth, we should ask ourselves, "Is Ellen White's use of a given Scripture text critical to her conclusion in a given statement?" If her application of a given Scripture is peripheral to her central theme it may not represent a thought-out exegesis. As is the case with Scripture, we are on safest ground when we refer to statements whose main intent is to address the issue we are concerned about.

When it comes to the book of Revelation her statements will be most helpful when the interpretation of a whole passage was the reason she was writing. If you want to know her view on Revelation 13, go to the statements where she systematically works through the chapter. On the other hand, much of the book of Revelation is never central to any of her discussions. We must exercise great caution in applying offhand and peripheral statements to our own interpretation of Revelation.[8]

5. Earlier or Later?

Fifth, we must allow Ellen White's later writings to explicate positions taken in earlier writings. As her writing skills increased, her ability to express accurately the thoughts she received from God increased correspondingly. And as earlier statements became subject to controversy, she would offer clarifying statements to make her intention clear. A well-known example of this is *Early Writings,* pages 85-96, in which she offers a series of clarifications of earlier statements and visionary descriptions.[9] So it is important to allow later statements regarding the biblical text to define her meaning in the earlier ones.

6. Singular or Frequent Usage?

Finally, how often did she utilize a scriptural passage in a particular way? All other things being equal, the number of times writers repeat a specific concept is in direct proportion to their passion for that topic to be clearly understood. It is not normally wise to base an interpretation on a single passage. An idea that reappears in a variety of circumstances and by means of a variety of expressions is not easily misunderstood or misused.

Ellen White and Exegesis

The main reason for suggesting these basic guidelines is the problem of ambiguity in Ellen White's writings. Her statements are often susceptible of more than one interpretation.[10] This is not a result of confusion or lack of clarity on her part necessarily, but rather of the fact that she often did not address directly the questions that concern us most today. An unbiased reader will repeatedly find statements that answer our concerns with less clarity than we would prefer. Biased readers, on the other hand, when confronted with an ambiguous statement, pick the option out of several that best fits their preconceived ideas and hammer it home to those who might disagree.

The reality is that we cannot clarify many exegetical questions from Ellen White's writings. The wisest course is to avoid using ambiguous statements as definitive evidence to prove a point. It is always appropriate, of course, to point out the possibilities inherent in such statements.

Conclusion

The nice thing about the interpretive strategies we have discussed in this chapter is that anyone can practice them. You don't need to have a Ph.D. or a specialized education in order to read the Bible accurately. If you follow these principles, you won't make the kind of mistakes that David Koresh and his followers made. These principles benefit anyone, even scholars of the Bible. In fact, if you know Greek and Hebrew, but you don't practice descriptive exegesis, pray, emphasize clear texts and general reading, or listen to others, there is a good chance that you will misunderstand the Bible regardless of how skillful your procedures are.

In the following chapters we apply these principles of exegesis in a practical way. I will show step by step how to uncover the intended meaning of the book of Revelation. This process will be more than just a dry overview of methods. Sample texts will come alive as we apply the methods. In the process we will discover some of the book of Revelation's best-kept secrets.

---

[1] "Those who are not walking in the light of the message may gather up statements from my writings that happen to please them, and that agree with their human judgment, and, by separating these statements from their connection and placing them beside human reasonings, make it appear that my writings uphold that which they condemn" (Ellen G. White letter 208, 1906).

[2] "Many from among our own people are writing to me, asking with earnest determination the privilege of using my writings to give force to certain subjects which they wish to present to the people in such a way as to leave a deep impression upon them. It is true that there is a reason why some of these matters should be presented; but I would not venture to give my approval in using the testimonies in this way, or to sanction the placing of matter which is good in itself in the way which they propose.

"The persons who make these propositions, for aught I know, may be able to conduct the enterprise of which they write in a wise manner; but nevertheless I dare not give the least license for using my writings in the manner which they propose. In taking account of such an enterprise, there are many things that must come into consideration; for in using the testimonies to bolster up some subject which may impress the mind of the author, the extracts may give a different impression than that which they would were they read in their original connection" ("The Writing and Sending Out of the *Testimonies for the Church,*" p. 26, in Arthur L. White, *Ellen G. White, Messenger to the Remnant,* p. 86).

[3] When she applied the phrase "touch not, taste not, handle not" to the use of tea, coffee, alcohol, and tobacco (*The Ministry of Healing,* p. 335), she was certainly echoing the language of Colossians 2:21, but certainly not in the manner in which Paul used it! For her the phrase had a positive use in relation to a proper abstention from harmful substances, but for Paul the phrase, in context, represented an unhealthy asceticism that diverted attention from Christ (Col. 2:18-23).

Or when she applied the phrase "God made man upright" to the need for good posture (*Education,* p. 198), she never intended to imply that the author of Ecclesiastes was discussing posture in Ecclesiastes 7:27-29. But in *Patriarchs and Prophets,* page 49, she used the phrase in harmony with the moral intention of the biblical author.

[4] See the illustration in the previous footnote for her use of Colossians 2:21.

[5] As mentioned in the previous chapter, a high percentage of her exegetical statements probably occur in *The Acts of the Apostles,* which contains specific discussions of New Testament books in their original setting. Many exegetical statements also appear in *Christ's Object Lessons* and *Thoughts From the Mount of Blessing.* Cf. the comments by Robert Olson in *Ministry* (December 1990, p. 17).

[6] Where Ellen White appears to employ a text exegetically, yet a tension remains between her use of a text and the apparent intent of the biblical author's language, we should keep two possibilities in mind. 1. It is possible that the interpreter has misunderstood the intent of either the biblical writer or Ellen White, or both. 2. An inspired person can apply a biblical passage to his or her contemporary situation in a local sense without exhausting the ultimate intention of the original writer. (Note Peter's use of Joel 2:28-32 in Acts 2:16-21, and Jesus' use of Daniel 7:13, 14 in Matthew 9:6.)

[7] *Testimonies for the Church,* vol. 5, p. 696; cf. *Selected Messages,* book 1, p. 66; *Testimonies to Ministers,* p. 33.

[8] Revelation is most central to her discussion in chapter 57 (pp. 579-592) of *The Acts of the Apostles* and to much of the latter part of *The Great Controversy.*

[9] A theological example of her maturing clarity of expression is her understanding of the deity of Christ. No one can mistake her clear belief in the full deity of Christ as expressed in later statements such as *Selected Messages,* book 1, p. 296; *The Desire of Ages,* p. 530; *Review and Herald,* Apr. 5, 1906; and *Signs of the Times,* May 3, 1899. But pre-1888 statements such as *The Spirit of Prophecy,* vol. 1, p. 17, 18 are ambiguous enough to be read as Arian if we ignore the later statements (she updates and clarifies *The Spirit of Prophecy,* reference in *Patriarchs and Prophets,* pp. 37, 38). To use *The Spirit of Prophecy,* vol. 1, pp. 17, 18 to demonstrate her view on the topic while ignoring the later clarifying statements is to hopelessly distort her intention.

[10] An excellent example of an ambiguous statement occurs in *Testimonies to Ministers,* p. 445. She states there that the "sealing of the servants of God [in Revelation 7] is the same that was shown to Ezekiel in vision. John also had been a witness of this most startling revelation." She follows with a number of items that are common to both books. Since the visions of John and Ezekiel are analogous but certainly not identical, two possibilities of interpretation emerge. 1. The events of around 600 B.C. partook of the same principles that will manifest themselves in the final crisis portrayed in Revelation 7. 2. Ezekiel describes not the events of 600 B.C. but the end-time. While one or the other interpretation will be considered more likely based on the prior assumptions a reader brings to the text, either is possible based on the language she chose to use in context.

5

TOOLS OF THE TRADE

About a decade ago I received a package from a pastor (let's call him George) that I respected a great deal. It contained a letter asking me to read the accompanying notebook on a highly difficult passage in the book of Revelation. George wanted my feedback on his research. Since I get many more such requests than I can handle, I laid the notebook aside at home, hoping to look at it sometime.

A couple nights later I was tossing and turning, completely unable to sleep. Not only did sleep elude me, my mind was crystal clear, as if I were wide awake and walking in the sunshine! Nothing is more boring than being wide awake in total darkness. It felt like solitary confinement! So I decided I might as well get up, go to the other end of the house, and quietly use that time in a useful way.

As I walked out to the living room, I remembered George's notebook. Going downstairs to my home office, I brought the notebook back upstairs, where it wasn't so chilly. As I read through his explanation of the passage, his logical presentation fascinated me. If I had not already spent 20 years on that passage I would have been completely convinced by his exposition. George wrote clearly and with passion. Yet for some reason, he saw something in each symbol and in each verse that my research indicated was not possible. It seemed to me that he was stringing a series of zeros together, believing that they added up to something. I thought it would not be difficult to set him straight.

Unlike other moments of apparent genius at 3:00 in the morning, the light of day did not change my opinion of George's notebook. So a few days later I sat down and wrote him a 15-page single-spaced letter. When he responded after a week or so, he hadn't bought a single thing I said! Back and forth the letters flew (funny how you can find time when the issue is interesting enough). No matter what either of us wrote, we didn't agree on a thing in the text!

Finally, one day it dawned on me what was happening. I was reading the book of Revelation as if it had been composed around AD. 90. He was approaching it as if it were written in A.D. 1990! Since it seemed rather obvious that John had authored Revelation in A.D. 90, I thought I had the smoking gun that would help him see my point of view. So I explained it to him in a letter. When he answered, it was the first time we agreed on anything. But was I ever in for a shock!

He explained to me his belief that as an Adventist he was obligated to read the book of Revelation as if written directly to Adventists. As if John were familiar with the writings of Ellen White and had spent time in *The Seventh-day Adventist Bible Commentary* and other Adventist books. And as if John were still a living prophet, speaking directly to the issues that drive Adventists in today's world.

I must confess that I remain fascinated with his logic and his honesty. While the participants in the 1919 Bible conference and most Adventist thought leaders since would have soundly rejected his position, he has maintained his conviction and continues to express it with clarity and passion. I remain, however, convinced that such a stance lies at the root of most misunderstanding of the book of Revelation.

No matter how one pretties things up, the reality is that the book of Revelation was not written in the past decade or even the past century. John composed it in the first century, and it speaks powerfully to that time and place. Everything we have covered so far in this book tells us that reading the book as if it directly addressed our personal situation is a surefire way to misinterpret its purpose and message. And I have noted through the years that Adventists who have taken George's position on Revelation rarely agree with each other. To read the Apocalypse from one's own point of view is to end up where you began—with ideas of your own making. In the chapter that follows I will begin to outline the path that will lead to an understanding of the book of Revelation in the context of its own time and place.

Revelation's Own Introduction

I would like to begin by asking the question "What does Revelation tell us about itself?" The best method for studying Revelation will be the one that emerges naturally from the text. We can learn a great deal about the book from its first four verses.

"The revelation of Jesus Christ, which *God gave* to him to show to his servants what must take place soon, and he *signified it* sending it through his angel to his servant John, who testified concerning the word of God and the testimony of Jesus Christ, which he saw. Blessed is the one who reads and *those who hear the words* of this prophecy, and who keep the things which are written in it, for the time is near.

"John, to the *seven churches which are in Asia:* Grace to you and peace from *the one being and the he was and the one coming,* and from the seven spirits which are before his throne" (Rev. 1:1-4).

The passage contains several clues about how the author himself would have wanted us to exegete the book of Revelation. Let me remind you that exegesis involves a couple things: seeking to understand what the writer was trying to say and holding open the possibility that we might learn something from the text. The text itself should govern what we see in it. What do these four verses tell us about a proper exegesis of Revelation?

A Christian Book

"The revelation of Jesus Christ, which God gave to him" (verse 1, NIV).

It is evident from the very first phrase ("the revelation of Jesus Christ") that it is a Christian book. Jesus Christ is present everywhere, both explicitly (Rev. 1:1, 2, 5, 9; 11:15; 12:10, 17; 14:12; 17:6; 19:10; 20:4, 6; 22:16, 20, 21) and in symbol (Rev. 1:12-16; 5:5ff.; 7:17; 12:5, 11; and 14:1ff., etc.). The book contains references to churches (Rev. 1-3 and 22:16) and to the cross (Rev. 1:18; 5:6, 9, 12; 11:8; 12:11). The careful reader also becomes aware that the book had scores if not hundreds of echoes of New Testament themes, vocabulary, and theology. As a result, although Revelation has a different style, vocabulary and subject matter than the rest of the New Testament, we should not expect its theology to be radically different than what we find there. It is the natural conclusion to the New Testament, the collection of books that forms the basis for Christian faith.

Let me give you a quick example: Revelation 9:2-6 has an incredibly strange description of locusts and scorpions tormenting people for five months. But if you compare Revelation 9 with Luke 10:17-20, you discover that the message of the two passages is the same—God takes care of His people in the face of a demonic plague. So even though the language is quite different than the rest of the New Testament, the theology is in harmony with the other 26 books of the New Testament. The book we are studying is a revelation of Jesus Christ, and we need to understand everything from that perspective.

A Divine Revelation

"The revelation of Jesus Christ, which *God gave* to him to show to his servants what must take place soon, and he signified it" (Rev. 1:1).

The second thing we can learn from Revelation 1:1-4 is that the book is a divine revelation ("God gave"). John repeatedly points to a supernatural origin for the scenes portrayed in his book (Rev. 1:10-20; 2:7, 11, etc.; 4:1; 10:11; 17:1-3; 19:9, 10; 22:6-10). He considers himself a prophet and his work a prophecy. The book of Revelation is more than just the work of a human writer, it is also the intention of a divine author. It is God through Jesus Christ who not only gives the visions but selects the symbols for this book ("and he signified it"). Revelation is more than just a human writer's intent. The vision is from God, therefore the words selected by John are also the words of God.

If the book comes from God, the meaning of Revelation will often go beyond what the human author might have understood. That, however, does not license interpreters to seek indiscriminately all kinds of extended meanings in the biblical text. Just as God limited Himself when He took on human nature in the incarnation, so He did the same when He chose to express Himself through the language of human authors in Scripture. Thus, whatever divine intent we may see in a passage should be a natural development of the human author's own language and purpose. In the text the divine intent and the human intent meet. Having discerned as far as possible the meaning of the human author's language, we are compelled by the divine claims of the book to ask what extended meaning God may have also placed in the text, to be revealed by history and subsequent revelation.

Relationship to Daniel

"The revelation of Jesus Christ, which God gave to him to show to his servants *what must take place soon,* and he signified it sending it through his angel to his servant John" (verse 1).

In his monumental commentary on the book of Revelation G. K. Beale demonstrates that the puzzling phrase "what must take place soon" is a deliberate allusion to Daniel 2.[1] There the prophet tells Nebuchadnezzar that the dream came to him because God wanted to "show him what must happen in the last days" (Dan. 2:28, author's translation from Greek Old Testament). By alluding to this text Revelation 1:1 seems to be saying that events Daniel promised would occur in the distant future were now getting under way and would be clarified in the book of Revelation. For Beale it means that the reader needs to understand the content of Revelation within the framework of Daniel 2 and its parallel apocalyptic prophecies, such as Daniel 7.

The author of Revelation seems to believe that a close relationship exists between the end times of Daniel and the prophecies of Revelation. The reader needs to lay the two books side by side. Their fundamental themes are similar. Because of the death and resurrection of Jesus (Rev. 1:5, 6; 3:21; 5:5) the great consummation of God's plans outlined in Daniel and Revelation is now secure, the final work of God is under way. To read Revelation without a strong awareness of the prophecies of Daniel would be a mistake.

The Language of Apocalyptic Symbolism

"The revelation of Jesus Christ, which God gave to him to show to his servants what must take place soon, and he *signified* it sending it through his angel to his servant John" (Rev. 1:1).

The very first verse of Revelation is a clear indication of symbolism in the book ("and he signified it"). In the rest of the Bible the normal procedure is to take things literally unless it becomes overwhelmingly clear that symbolism is intended. Studying Revelation, on the other hand, calls for the opposite strategy. In Revelation one approaches things symbolically unless the passages overwhelmingly require a literal understanding.

But even a cursory reading of Revelation reveals that the symbolism of the book is out of the ordinary. At times it is even rather bizarre. The book describes animals that do not look anything like the kind you find in the forest. In addition, it contains numerous symbols and concepts that are foreign to normal life. For example, it mentions beasts with seven heads and 10 horns. If you ever saw something like that in the forest you would know you had been drinking! One of the seven-headed, 10-horned beasts even had feet like a bear, a body like a leopard, and a mouth like a lion. Such an animal does not exist in the real world.

But while such symbolism may seem strange to us at first, it was fairly common in the ancient world. A book called 1 Enoch (or Ethiopic Enoch), written perhaps 100 years before the time of Jesus, has seven archangels, including Gabriel and Michael. The book of Revelation has archangels as well, and they usually number seven. Enoch also has a heavenly city with 12 gates, three on each of four sides. Another book, called The Apocalypse of Zephaniah, a Jewish writing of the first century, has a remarkable description that is similar to that in the book of Revelation:

"Then I arose and stood, and I saw a great angel standing before me with his face shining like the rays of the sun in its glory since his face is like that which is perfected in its glory. And he was girded as if a golden girdle were upon his breast. His feet were like bronze which is melted in a fire. And when I saw him, I rejoiced, for I thought that the Lord Almighty had come to visit me. I fell upon my face, and I worshiped him. He said to me, 'Take heed. Don't worship me. I am not the Lord Almighty but I am the great angel—Eremiel, who is over the abyss and Hades, the one in which all of the souls are imprisoned from the end of the Flood, which came upon the earth, until this day"(Apocalypse of Zephaniah 6:11-15).

A number of elements in this description remind me of the vision of Jesus found in Revelation 1. Apocalyptic was a style of writing in the ancient world, one that communicated very clearly in those days. So while the language of Revelation is often bizarre, the first century reader had a context in which to interpret it. What I find exciting is that this apocalyptic style is becoming increasingly popular in today's world. Movies such as *The Lion King, Armageddon,* and *The Matrix* apply apocalyptic themes and images to life as we know it. This suggests to me that the book of Revelation has never been more relevant than it is today.

The Churches of Asia

"John, to the *seven churches which are in Asia*" (Rev. 1:4).

The third point that we gather from Revelation 1:1-4 is that the book is set in Asia Minor, that the churches belong to the Roman Province of Asia. This should not surprise us since we spent some time on the book's setting in the first chapter. The question is Was Revelation written for a later time, or did its author intend that its original audience also understand it? The answer appears in verse 3.

"Blessed is the one who reads and *those who hear the words* of this prophecy, and who keep the things which are written in it, for the time is near." The emphasized words translate a Greek expression that implies "hear with understanding." In other words, God and His human author, John, intended the book of Revelation to be understood. This differs from the book of Daniel, in which a significant portion of the book was sealed up, not meant to be understood:

"I, Daniel, was exhausted and lay ill for several days. Then I got up and went about the king's business. I was appalled by the vision; it was beyond understanding" (Dan. 8:27, NIV).

"'But you, Daniel, close up and seal the words of the scroll until the time of the end. Many will go here and there to increase knowledge'" (Dan.12:4, NIV).

The book of Daniel thus contained some things not understood by the original author or the original audience. But that is not the case with the book of Revelation.

The Greek verb for "hearing" (Rev. 1:3) has two possible implications: you can hear *without* understanding or you can hear *with* understanding. Revelation 1:3 combines the verb "hear" with an object ("the words") in the accusative case, and that means that understanding accompanies the "hearing." In other words, the book of Revelation was not sealed up for some future time, but was intended to be heard and understood even by its first audience.

So the book of Revelation tracks with the concept we learned in chapter 2, *God meets people where they are.* God dealt with John where he was. In the process He used some of the live symbols of his day. The book is set in the Asia Minor of the first century and makes the most sense in that context.

Let me give you an example of what I mean by a "live symbol." Revelation 1 presents a glorious picture of Jesus. The source of all that John receives in his vision, He has the keys of hell and of death, is the Beginning and the End, the First and the Last, sends His angels to guide John, etc. A surprising connection exists between these images and the ancient setting of Asia Minor.

An ancient goddess named Hekate enjoyed great popularity in western Asia Minor. People in those days thought of the universe as a three-story building—heaven was at the top, hell was below, and in between was the earth where people lived. Hekate had the keys of both heaven and hell. She could travel back and forth between the three "stories," reporting to earth what was going on in the other two. Also she was known as "The Beginning and the End" and used angels to transmit her messages. Can you see the parallels between Hekate and Jesus? John seems to be telling the pagans of Asia Minor that the true source of revelation, the true holder of the keys, was not Hekate, but Jesus. All that they had sought from Hekate, they would actually find in Him.

It seems clear, then, that the book of Revelation reflected things going on in the real world of Asia Minor. Revelation was not isolated from its environment, but was written in the language of that time and place. The question naturally arises: "Why would an inspired writer use pagan concepts? What purpose would there be in describing Jesus in the language of a pagan goddess?"

I think there are two reasons. First of all, since it was part of their thought world, such language communicated to people who lived in a pagan culture. It made sense to them. Second, inspired writers might use pagan language to do battle with pagan theology. If you are going to oppose other ideas around you, you need to speak the language in which those ideas come. So the book of Revelation is more than just a letter to the churches—it also enters into a dialogue with the ancient non-Christian world. The book addresses the time and place of first century Asia Minor.

The Grammar of Revelation

"John, to the seven churches which are in Asia: Grace to you and peace from *the one being and the he was and the one coming,* and from the seven spirits which are before his throne" (verse 4).

My translation of verse 4 is an attempt to show how the grammar of Revelation would have struck the original readers. The greeting at the beginning of the book originates from the One "who is and was and is to come." But in the Greek, the language is an unnatural combination of participles with a finite verb. That's why I translated it: "From the one being, and the he was, and the one coming." That is not good English grammar, and it is even worse Greek grammar. So right at the beginning of the book you run into this incredible construction that would stop any Greek-speaking person in his or her tracks. What is going on here? Is the writer of the book uneducated? Is he translating in his mind from some other language? Or is this some sort of "language of heaven"?

In the introduction we briefly examined several possibilities. Probably the best explanation is that John was not from a Greek background and did not have access to expert editorial help while on Patmos. The Greek of Revelation comes across like the immature writing on a child's school tablet. The good news, though, is that God can use anyone even though they are not an expert in the language of the day. Revelation brought a powerful message to God's people even though the style is at times ungrammatical.

Use of the Old Testament

Moving beyond Revelation 1:1-4, a careful reading of the whole book exposes the importance of the Old Testament to the book's visions. To quote William Milligan, a commentator on the book:

"The book of Revelation is absolutely steeped in the memories, the incidents, the thought, and the language of the church's past. To such an extent is this the case that it may be doubted whether it contains a single figure not drawn from the Old Testament, or a single complete sentence not more or less built up of materials brought from the same source."[2]

We noticed this point in chapter 2, when we briefly examined Revelation 13. Perhaps 2,000 words, concepts, and ideas in Revelation touch base with the Old Testament in one form or another. Knowledge of the Old Testament becomes the key to the code of Revelation. If you do not know the Old Testament, you will have little hope of understanding Revelation.

But John's use of the Old Testament is a bit complicated. The book of

Revelation never quotes the Hebrew Scriptures. It only alludes to them with a hint here and there or a word here and a phrase there. Because of this we need to examine the use of the Old Testament in Revelation very carefully. It is important not to miss those places in the book where the author intends readers to make a connection with some Old Testament passage. On the other hand, it is crucial not to manufacture parallels where none exist. So any method we might develop for the study of Revelation must give serious attention to how one determines allusions to the Old Testament.

Repetitive Structure

Another thing that is fairly obvious as you work your way through Revelation is its highly repetitive structure. Thus we notice seven churches, seven seals, seven trumpets, and seven bowls. Furthermore, as you compare the trumpets and the bowls, you see tremendous parallels between them. The first trumpet affects the earth (Rev. 8:7), while the first bowl also has an impact on the earth (Rev. 16:2). The second trumpet affects the sea (Rev 8:8, 9), as does the second bowl (Rev. 16:3). The sixth trumpet and the sixth bowl both deal with the Euphrates River (Rev. 9:14; 16:12), and so on. In addition, we find numerous parallels between the opening section of Revelation and the verses at the close (Rev. 1:1-8; 22:6-21). So any method that hopes to unlock the secrets of the book of Revelation will need to give careful attention to the book's structure.

Scenes of Worship

Finally, a surprising aspect of the book of Revelation is the constant reference to worship. In spite of all the strange beasts, violence, and military language, the book of Revelation is never complete without some mention of divine worship. It is almost impossible to read through the book and not notice how central worship is. Revelation is full of hymns, images of the sanctuary, and scenes of worship. Notice this glorious example of heavenly worship.

"And when he had taken it, the four living creatures and the twenty-four elders *fell down before the Lamb*. Each one had a harp and they were holding *golden bowls full of incense, which are the prayers of the saints. And they sang a new song:*

"'You are worthy to take the scroll and to open its seals, because you were slain, and with your blood you purchased men for God from every tribe and language and people and nation. You have made them to be a kingdom and priests to serve our God, and they will reign on earth.'

"Then I looked and heard the voice of many angels, numbering thousands upon thousands, and ten thousand times ten thousand. They encircled the throne and the living creatures and the elders. *In a loud voice they sang:*

"'Worthy is the Lamb, who was slain, to receive power and wealth and wisdom and strength and honor and glory and praise!'

"Then I heard every creature in heaven and on earth and under the earth and on the sea, and all that is in them, *singing:*

"'To him who sits on the throne and to the Lamb be praise and honor and glory and power, for ever and ever!'*

"The four living creatures said, 'Amen,' and *the elders fell down and worshiped*" (Rev. 5:8-14, NIV).

Basic Exegetical Strategies

The goal of the observations we have been making is to help us to understand how the author of Revelation intends us to exegete, or interpret, the book. What I would like to do here, and in the chapters to come, is develop these observations into practical steps that draw out the meaning of Revelation. In the rest of this chapter we will briefly cover the first main step, doing basic exegesis of the text. Its goal is to determine as far as possible what the author intended by writing it. Basic exegesis is the kind of approach one would follow with any part of the Bible. It includes procedures such as the following.

Looking for Key Words

It is helpful to begin by reading the chosen passage through several times in a variety of translations. After all, the book of Revelation pronounces a blessing on those who read it (Rev. 1:3)! As you go through the passage make a list of the difficulties in it that you need to resolve. In particular you will want to identify the words that require special study. Note ones that have major theological meaning in other parts of the Bible or ones that are unclear at first glance. Especially pay attention to those words that appear repeatedly in the passage. Basic to any exegesis of a text is understanding the key terms that the writer was using.

When you have identified the important words in the passage, you will want to discover the range of meaning each one can have. For starters, you can turn to Bible dictionaries or lexicons to discover their semantic range. If you don't know Greek, you can still touch base with the original language by finding the word in a Greek-English lexicon. Use an interlinear Bible or an analytical concordance (such as Young's or Strong's) to determine the form of the Greek word; then look it up. Concordances can be helpful here as well. You can discover how other parts of the Bible use a key word, how it functioned in a variety of contexts. Give particular attention to how the same author employs the word elsewhere. This process is similar to learning the biblical language in context, the way a child acquires language. Let's look at an example of this kind of word study.

"The revelation of Jesus Christ, which God gave him to show his servants what must soon take place. He *made it known* by sending his angel to his servant John" (Rev. 1:1, NIV) This is one time when the translation does not help us. The phrase "made it known" reflects a word that we can also render "signified." "He signified it by sending his angel to his servant John."

If you look up the Greek word for "signified" in other parts of the New Testament (Acts 11:28; John 12:33, 18:32, and 21:19), you will find that it has a very particular connotation. It means something like "a cryptic saying or action that points to a future event." So Revelation is a signified book, it is a volume full of symbolic sayings and actions that point to future events. The author of Revelation here defines the whole book in one word.

The New International Version lets us down here by offering an interpretive phrase that is somewhat helpful but leaves the reader with no clue about the original word. So this is one of those times when using a variety of translations can help you see that the translation is more interpretive than literal. Then you can use a lexicon or a concordance to develop your own understanding of the word. Once you have established the range of meaning the word could have, you will want to determine which connotation the author intended in the context of the passage you are studying.

Examining the word for "signified" has provided an important payoff. Many people believe that when you are studying the Bible, you should always take the text literally unless it becomes obvious that a symbol is intended. And this is generally true, when it comes to the Gospels or the letters of Paul. But in Revelation the opposite seems to be the case. It is not a literal book but a signified book. It is in most cases to be taken symbolically.

Looking for Key Words

1. Read the passage you are examining several times.
2. Determine the key words.
   - ✔ Unusual words
   - ✔ Words of uncertain meaning
   - ✔ Words crucial to understanding
   - ✔ Words used repeatedly
3. Discover the range of meaning for each key word.
   - ✔ Determine the original word with an interlinear or analytical concordance.
   - ✔ Look the word up in a lexicon or Bible dictionary.
   - ✔ Use a concordance to see how other texts use the word.
4. Determine the specific meaning in the context of your passage.

How Words Relate to Each Other

The second step in basic exegesis is what scholars would call "syntax." The word has nothing to do with taxes on prostitution or alcohol! Rather the syntax involves how word pairs affect each other's meaning. When we place two words in relationship with one another the meaning of both words often changes. So it is important to consider how major words in a passage influence each other.

So once again read through the passage several times. Identify words and combinations of words that require a decision between two or more options. Consider those options in the light of similar usages elsewhere in the book and in the author's other writings. Let's look at an example or two of how this works.

The book of Revelation begins with the phrase "the revelation of Jesus" (Rev. 1:1). What exactly does this phrase mean? Is it a revelation that comes "from" Jesus? Or is it "about" Jesus? That is an example of a syntactical question. Both options are possible based on the grammar of the phrase. Interpreters may make an arbitrary decision about the passage without thinking about other options. But that limits the possibilities of the text. An arbitrary answer may satisfy, but it may nevertheless be wrong.

Is the revelation of Jesus something that comes from Jesus or is it something that tells us about Jesus? Both possibilities may be true. But in the case of Revelation 1:1 the emphasis seems to be on a revelation "from" Jesus. The text offers a chain of revelation moving from God to Jesus to John to the churches. The point of the passage is the origin of the vision more than its content.

Another example. What is "the testimony of Jesus"? Is it a testimony that Jesus gives? Or is it one that someone else presents "about" Jesus? Great treasures of meaning can lurk behind such simple questions. In the case of Revelation, scholarship indicates that the normal usage of the "sub-jective-objective genitive" of "testimony" is subjective. In other words, the testimony of Jesus is one that Jesus bears, just as "the word of their testimony" (Rev. 12:11) is a testimony given by the overcomers—it is not one about them.

In summary, once you have identified and defined the key words in a passage, you will want to determine what alternatives to understanding the various combinations of words offer to our interpretation of the text. You will want to consider the options in the light of similar phrases elsewhere in the book or even in the Bible as a whole. Then you will want to decide, as far as possible, how we should interpret the phrase in the specific passage you are studying. Often such word relationships can be quite clear in a specific context. At other times we may never know for sure.

Sentences and Their Context

A third step in basic exegesis is grammar. Grammar, in the narrow sense, is the study of how words and groups of words relate to each other in sentences and ultimately in paragraphs. Are the nouns in a passage the subject or object of the verb? What is the main sentence? What words or phrases are in a subordinate relationship to the main sentence? Is the main verb present, past, or future tense, and what difference does that make? What role do the adjectives and adverbs play in the sentence? For those who have learned the skill, diagramming sentences can be an effective tool for biblical understanding. Some books recommend what is called a "syntactical display." See the bibliography at the end of the chapter for further resources.

It should go without saying, perhaps, that the more faithful and exact the translation you are working with, the more productive this step can be. In the English language the Bibles most faithful to the grammar of the original text are the King James Version, the American Standard Version, and the *New American Standard Bible*. Working with the grammar can be difficult for many people but practice develops the skill. The more we grow in the use of grammatical tools, the better our understanding of the biblical authors' intentions.

As you work with a biblical text it is helpful to determine its boundaries. Where do paragraphs begin and end? A paragraph is a group of sentences focused on a single main idea. You can usually mark off a paragraph at the point where a new sentence takes off on a different theme or idea. By using a variety of translations, you can compare how others have marked off the paragraphs in your chosen passage. Where all translations agree, there is reasonable certainty. But where you find disagreement among translations, you will need to wrestle with the options for yourself. A phrase such as "after these things" (Rev. 4:1) or "and I saw" (Rev. 5:1; 6:1) may mark off the larger scenes in the book. Once again the chapter and section divisions of the major translations can provide a guide to a tentative assessment of boundaries. Further exegetical work of your own can help you come to a more final decision.

Sentences and Their Context

1. Choose a version of the Bible that is faithful to the grammar of the original.
   - ✔ King James Version
   - ✔ American Standard Version
   - ✔ *New American Standard Bible*
2. Determine subject, object, and subordinate clauses in each sentence.
3. Try diagramming sentences or using a "syntactical display" (see bibliography).
4. Determine the boundaries of each paragraph.
   - ✔ Compare your insights with a variety of translations.
5. Determine the boundaries of larger scenes.

The Ancient Background of the Text

Finally, and perhaps most difficult for the lay scholar, is determining the background (the historical, literary, and cultural setting) of the book. In the case of Revelation, the setting in Asia Minor, the live symbols that would have affected people there, the apocalyptic language, the gods they worshiped, etc., are examples of the kinds of things that lie in the background of any ancient writing. But many assume such topics to be the domain of specialists. How can the average person get at those things without obtaining specialized training in the history and culture of the first-century world?

You can begin with a general encyclopedia, a Bible encyclopedia, or encyclopedias of the Roman world, learning all you can about the Roman Empire and first-century Asia Minor. It is good to start with the big picture. Bible dictionaries, then, will often contain articles discussing various aspects of this background. Critical commentaries, such as the one by

---

The Ancient Background of the Text

1. Read articles about the Roman world in encyclopedias and Bible dictionaries.
2. Look up the passage you are studying in a critical commentary or two.
   - ✔ David Aune: *Word Biblical Commentary*
   - ✔ G. K. Beale: *New International Greek Testament Commentary*
   - ✔ R. H. Charles: *International Critical Commentary*
   - ✔ Ranko Stefanovic: his commentary from Andrews University Press
   - ✔ *The Seventh-day Adventist Bible Commentary* introductory articles in volumes 5-7
3. Use the bibliographies and references in the above as a guide to further understanding.
4. Become familiar with translations of some of the nonbiblical apocalypses.
   - ✔ Ethiopic Enoch (1 Enoch)
   - ✔ 4 Ezra (2 Esdras)
   - ✔ The Apocalypse of Zephaniah
   - ✔ 2 Baruch

David Aune in the *Word Biblical Commentary,* will connect the passage you are studying with information about the goddess Hekate or parallel passages in ancient books such as 1 Enoch and The Apocalypse of Zephaniah.[3] While you don't ever want to treat commentaries as the voice of God, some knowledge of the background will help you to make wise judgments about the text and its context. The introductory articles in the *The Seventh-day Adventist Bible Commentary* offer another good source of information about the ancient world.

Ultimately, you will find it worthwhile to use the sources at your disposal to try answering questions about the historical, literary, and cultural setting of the book, questions such as the following: For what kind of audience was the book originally intended? What was the author's purpose for the book as a whole? What can we know about the landscape and the climate, and how does that affect the way the author may have composed the book? What was the political and religious situation of the recipients of the book? What other writings of the time might give us some clues to the message of Revelation? And how did people of the time live and support themselves?

Conclusion

The procedures that we have just outlined are typical of the approach one ought to take toward any biblical text. If you want to understand what an author was trying to say, the basic steps include: looking at the words and the relationships between words; examining the larger structure of sentences and paragraphs; and then asking questions about background and trying to understand the significance of the text within that background. This type of approach will be successful in unlocking most parts of the Bible. If you can figure out what Paul was trying to say in Romans, for example, you will have understood Paul.

But this approach does not work as well in the book of Revelation. Actually, it is not difficult to understand what the author was trying to say. The problem is that even when you know what John said, you still have almost no idea what he meant. A classic example of this is the first trumpet (Rev. 8:7): "The first angel sounded his trumpet, and there came hail and fire mixed with blood, and it was hurled down upon the earth. A third of the earth was burned up, a third of the trees were burned up, and all the green grass was burned up" (NIV).

It isn't hard to figure out what the author states here. He said that *an angel sounded his trumpet, fire mixed with blood was thrown to the earth, burning up a third of the earth and trees as well as all the green grass.* The problem is that while you know what he was trying to say, you still have no idea what he actually meant by it. So the basic strategies of exegesis are inadequate by themselves to unveil the meaning of Revelation.

Based on the characteristics drawn from Revelation at the beginning of this chapter, understanding the book requires a broader, more theological method of exegesis. We cannot limit ourselves to methods that might work just fine for Matthew or for Romans. Instead, we need to develop a method of exegesis appropriate for the book of Revelation. Revelation will not reveal its secrets without three further steps that we will cover in the final three chapters of this book. These steps include careful attention (1) to the structure of Revelation, (2) to its Old Testament background, and (3) to how the gospel transforms Old Testament images in the light of what Jesus has done. The following chapter is an exciting look at the structure of Revelation and the way it helps to unpack the book's secrets.

Resources on the "How to" of Biblical Exegesis

Bock, Darrell L. "New Testament Word Analysis." In *Introducing New Testament Interpretation.* Ed. Scot McKnight. Guides to New Testament Exegesis. Grand Rapids: Baker Book House, 1989. Pp. 97-113.

Gugliotto, Lee J. *Handbook for Bible Study.* Hagerstown, Md.: Review and Herald Publishing Association, 1995.

Heard, Warren. "New Testament Background." In *Introducing New Testament Interpretation.* Ed. Scot McKnight. Guides to New Testament Exegesis. Grand Rapids: Baker Book House, 1989. Pp. 21-51.

Fee, Gordon D. *New Testament Exegesis: A Handbook for Students and Pastors,* rev. ed. Louisville: Westminster/John Knox Press, 1993.

Kaiser, Walter C., Jr. *Toward an Exegetical Theology: Biblical Exegesis for Preaching and Teaching.* Grand Rapids: Baker Book House, 1981.

Liefeld, Walter L. *New Testament Exposition.* Grand Rapids: Zondervan Pub. House, 1984.

McKnight, Scot. "New Testament Greek Grammatical Analysis." In *Introducing New Testament Interpretation.* Ed. Scot McKnight. Guides to New Testament Exegesis (Grand Rapids: Baker Book House, 1989. Pp. 75-97.

Michaels, J. Ramsey. *Interpreting the Book of Revelation*. Ed. Scot McKnight. Guides to New Testament Exegesis. Grand Rapids: Baker Book House, 1992. Pp. 89-94.

---

[1] G. K. Beale, *The Book of Revelation,* ed. by I. Howard Marshall and Donald A. Hagner, New International Greek Testament Commentary (Grand Rapids: Eerdmans, 1999), pp. 153, 154.

[2] William Milligan, *Lectures on the Apocalypse* (London: MacMillan and Co., 1892), p. 72.

[3] These books and many others have been translated into English in James H. Charlesworth, *The Old Testament Pseudepigrapha: Apocalyptic Literature and Testaments* (Garden City, N.Y.: Doubleday, 1983), vol. 1.

6

THE STRUCTURE
OF REVELATION

In most books of the New Testament the structure flows continuously from beginning to end. The primary context of any passage is the material that comes just before and just after. In Revelation, however, things are different. We find an interlocking complexity to the structure of Revelation that is astounding. The primary context of a given passage may be in a totally different part of the book. So in Revelation the immediate context is not always as crucial as it is for other books of the New Testament. *We should think of the primary context of most passages in Revelation as being the book as a whole.* Parallel words, ideas, and structures at the opposite end of the book may be as vital to understanding a passage as its immediate context.

So the structure of Revelation is of even greater importance than is usually the case in the New Testament. In this chapter we discover some special literary strategies the author introduced to help the reader gain a clearer understanding of the book. The strategies we will explore here are repetitive structures, duodirectionality, chiastic parallels, and the use of the Old Testament sanctuary as a structuring device. Discovering such strategies will not be merely an academic exercise—they help unlock the deep things of the book.

Repetitive Structures

The book of Revelation contains a number of repetitive structures. Among other things, you will find several groupings of seven: seven churches, seven seals, seven trumpets, and seven bowls (often known as the "seven last plagues"). John has also seven beatitudes ("Blessed are") scattered through the book. When you discover parallel structures, it's helpful to notice both the parallels and the contrasts. If one of the parallel structures is clearer than the other, the clear one can help to explain the ambiguous one. This is an invaluable tool for studying some of the most difficult passages. By way of example, let's look at the trumpets (Rev. 8–11) and the bowls (Rev. 16).

"The first angel sounded his trumpet, and there came hail and fire mixed with blood, and it was hurled down upon *the earth.* A third of *the earth* was burned up, a third of the trees were burned up, and all the green grass was burned up" (Rev. 8:7, NIV).

Compare the first trumpet with the first bowl of wrath:

"The first angel went and poured out his bowl on *the land,* and ugly and painful sores broke out on the people who had the mark of the beast and worshiped his image" (Rev. 16:2, NIV).

According to the New International Version the first trumpet falls on "the earth" and the first bowl falls on "the land." Both terms, however, are actually translating the same Greek word. So the first trumpet and the first bowl both affect the earth. But the parallels between the trumpets and the bowls go much further than this.

"The second angel sounded his trumpet, and something like a huge mountain, all ablaze, was thrown into the *sea.* A third of *the sea turned into blood,* a third of the *living creatures* in the sea died, and a third of the ships were destroyed" (Rev. 8:8, 9, NIV).

Compare the second trumpet with the second bowl.

"The second angel poured out his bowl on the *sea,* and *it turned into blood* like that of a dead man, and every *living thing* in the sea died" (Rev. 16:3, NIV).

Notice that the second trumpet and second bowl both fall on the sea and in both cases water turns into blood. While masked in translation, both verses use the Greek word for "soul" to describe creatures in the sea. So we observe a very strong parallel between these two passages. Notice also the interesting contrast. In both of the trumpets we have examined the plague falls on a "third" of the earth. A third of the earth burns up (Rev. 8:7), a third of the sea turns into blood (verse 8), a third of the ships get destroyed (verse 9), and so on. But in the seven bowls the plagues affect the whole earth. Everyone who has the mark of the beast suffers from the first bowl (Rev. 16:2). Every living thing in the sea dies (verse 3). So there are both parallels and contrasts. The trumpets and the bowls are very similar, yet they are also quite different.

If you continue working through the comparison, the third trumpet and bowl both fall on the springs of water, the fourth in each case strikes the heavens, the fifth trumpet and bowl produce darkness, the sixth both affect the Euphrates, and the seventh each result in the consummation of all things. While there are differences, the trumpets and the bowls are deliberately parallel in terms of their language and their content. This insight can be very helpful to an interpreter.

Most people studying the book of Revelation feel that the seven bowls are easier to understand than the seven trumpets. If that is the case, the information that you gain through a study of the bowls you can then apply to your exploration of the trumpets. By comparing passages that are eight chapters apart, one can gain information that works both ways. One thing that seems obvious in the bowls section is that they fall exclusively on the enemies of God and His people. The parallel between the trumpets and the bowls help confirm that the trumpets also focus exclusively on the wicked. Repetitive structures, therefore, provide clues to the deeper meanings that the author has placed in the book.

Finding Repetitive Structures

1. Choose a version of the Bible that is faithful to the grammar of the original.

    ✔ King James Version

    ✔ American Standard Version

    ✔ *New American Standard Bible*

2. When using a concordance or Bible margins, look for potential parallel texts in Revelation.

3. Where you encounter a significant number of words and ideas that are clearly parallel, you have a potential parallel structure.

4. Notice also the points of contrast between the parallel passages.

5. Evaluate the theological impact on both passages.

6. Where one passage is clearer than the other, move from the clear to the unclear.

There are a couple of other major parallel structures I'd like to mention at this point. Still others will make their appearance in the discussion of chiastic structures. A surprising parallel emerges when you compare what Revelation declares about end-time Babylon in chapters 17, 18, and 19 with what it says about the New Jerusalem in chapters 21 and 22. John compares the golden city with the city of doom, the bride with the prostitute. The New Jerusalem proves to be everything that Babylon failed to be. Citizens of Babylon, therefore, are excluded from the New Jerusalem. One further surprising parallel emerges when you compare the two witnesses of Revelation 11:3-6 with the land beast of 13:11-18.

Duodirectionality: Looking Both Ways

That brings us to a second type of structural tactic in the book of Revelation, which for lack of a better description, I have called duodirectionality. It is a fancy term that means transitional passages in the book of Revelation often look both forward and backward (people who study a lot develop fancy terms so they can quickly understand each other). Such duodirectional passages summarize what has gone before but at the same time point forward to what is yet to come.

Maybe I could put it a different way. In most books a writer introduces a chapter, adds the main content, and then places a conclusion at the end of the chapter. The writer then puts an introduction at the beginning of the next chapter, and so on. But the author of Revelation, whether one thinks of God or John in that role, seems to have developed a special tactic in presenting the vision. In the book of Revelation the introduction to what follows is very often embedded in the conclusion that precedes it. To notice this is to find the author's own explanation of what follows hidden in what precedes. But to ignore it is to miss the author's own commentary or interpretation of what follows. Discovering this principle, therefore, makes a major difference in our understanding of the deep things in the text. We'll look at a couple examples here.

Revelation 3:21

Revelation 3:21 is the verse that brought the principle of duodirectionality to my attention more than 10 years ago. "To him who overcomes, I will give the right to sit with me on my throne, just as I overcame and sat

down with my Father on his throne" (NIV). The passage is clearly the climax of the letters to the seven churches. Each of the seven churches receives a promise to the "overcomer." The one who overcomes will receive
specific rewards. What I find especially interesting is that the overcomer
promises are progressive. The first church (Ephesus) gets one promise (Rev.
2:7), the second (Smyrna) two (Rev. 2:10, 11), and so on, until the sixth
church (Philadelphia) receives six whole promises (Rev. 3:10-12)! So there
is a clear intensification as you work through the seven overcomer promises.

The seventh overcomer promise, in verse 21, is clearly the promise to
end all promises! Not only is it the seventh in the sequence of seven, it is
the climax and conclusion of all the others. After all, once you are sitting
on the throne of God you have everything God could give! The seventh
promise to the churches sums up and includes all the other promises. So
Revelation 3:21 is clearly the climax point of the seven letters in
Revelation 2 and 3.

But like Revelation 1:19, this passage is more than just a conclusion to
what has come before. It also contains ideas that set the stage for the next
section, the heavenly throne vision leading up to the opening of the seven
seals (Rev. 4:1-8:1). Let's look at Revelation 3:21 again, but this time in
my own translation that expresses more of the nuances in the original
Greek. "To the one who *overcomes* I *will give* to sit with me on my throne,
even as I also *overcame,* and *sat down* with my Father on His throne."

The "even as" (underlined) divides the verse into two parts, the first
focusing on the overcoming of the believer and the second on the overcoming of Jesus Christ. The text clearly relates the experience of the believer with that of Jesus. Both go through a time of overcoming and both
received a reward on the throne (all four elements are in italics in the text).
But particularly interesting is the fact that the section of Revelation that
follows this verse uniquely features each element.

Where in the book of Revelation do you encounter the Father's
throne? It's in chapter 4. Jesus joins the Father on His throne in chapter 5,
and the redeemed join Jesus on His throne in chapter 7 (verses 15-17). Each
aspect is a crucial piece of the following section, one of the most difficult to
understand in the whole book of Revelation. Revelation 3:21 contains in
a nutshell the substance of what is to follow in chapters 4, 5, and 7. *It is as
if John had buried the key to the seven seals in the climax of the seven churches.*

What portion of the seven seals does the phrase "the one who overcomes" summarize? It would seem to point ahead to chapter 6, which opens up the seals one at a time. The unfolding of the seals is all about the overcoming of the people of God in the course of Christian history. So in the very conclusion to the seven churches we find a nutshell synopsis of the key themes of chapters 4-7.

According to Revelation 3:21 the main story line of the seals has to do with God's people and the process by which they overcome here on earth. John models the overcoming of God's people on the overcoming of Jesus (Rev. 5:5). And just as His enthronement with the Father (Rev. 5:6-14) follows Jesus' overcoming, so the overcoming of God's people will receive as its reward a secure place in the temple of God forever (Rev. 7:15-17).

The principle of duodirectionality, therefore, uncovers a basic literary strategy of the author of Revelation. The author has embedded at the conclusion of the previous section material that offers a concise summary of the seven seals themselves. One reason people have had so much difficulty understanding the seven seals is because they have missed the author's own clues to the meaning of that vision. When we look carefully at the material in the previous sections of Revelation we will gain much information about the visions that follow.

The Fifth Seal (Rev. 6:9-11)

Let's look at one more interesting example of duodirectionality. The fifth seal (Rev. 6:9-11) functions as a climax to the four horses of Revelation 6:1-8 and summarizes their overall effect. The horses graphically express the suffering of God's people:

"When he opened the fifth seal, I saw under the altar the souls of those who *had been slain* because of the word of God and the testimony they had maintained. They called out in a loud voice, *'How long,* Sovereign Lord, holy and true, until you judge *the inhabitants of the earth* and avenge our blood?'" (Rev. 6:9, 10, NIV).

In the context of the four horsemen God's people have endured a great deal. Their experience resulted in the many martyrs pictured under the altar. They raise the poignant issue of how long God will delay his judgment on those who have persecuted them. Note that the cause of their suffering is "the inhabitants of the earth." They seem to be saying, "How long, O Lord, will you hold back from passing just judgment on the ones who martyred us?" Once again, a summary passage looks forward to what follows in the book of Revelation. The cry of the saints finds an echo in Revelation 8:13:

"As I watched, I heard an eagle that was flying in midair call out in a loud voice: 'Woe! Woe! Woe to *the inhabitants of the earth,* because of the trumpet blasts about to be sounded by the other three angels!'" (Rev. 8:13, NIV)."The inhabitants of the earth" is the key phrase of Revelation 6:10, the climax of the four horsemen! Apparently, in the book of Revelation "the inhabitants of the earth" is a way of describing those who trouble and persecute God's people. The cry goes out in Revelation 6:10 and receives its answer in Revelation 8:13. The trumpets of Revelation 8 and 9 are about what God is doing to judge those who have persecuted His saints.

A look at the introduction to the trumpets (Rev. 8:3, 4) makes the connection between the trumpets and the fifth seal ever firmer:

"Another angel, who had a golden censer, came and stood *at the altar.* He was given much incense to offer, with *the prayers of all the saints,* on the golden altar before the throne. The smoke of the incense, together with the prayers of the saints, went up before God from the angel's hand" (NIV).

Once again we find mention of the altar, presumably the same one as in the fifth seal. Where in Revelation do we find the prayers of the saints? In the fifth seal! Those prayers begin to ascend as the saints cry out in Revelation 6:9, 10. Then in Revelation 8:3 the prayers rise up from earth and come before the heavenly altar. Notice how God responds to them.

"Then the angel took the censer, filled it with fire from the altar, and hurled it on the earth; and there came peals of thunder, rumblings, flashes of lightning and an earthquake. Then the seven angels who had the seven trumpets prepared to sound them" (Rev. 8:5, 6, NIV).

God's answer to the prayers of the saints is to ready the seven trumpet angels to hurl judgments down to the earth. This sequence is tremendously important. The seven trumpets are perhaps the most difficult passage in the book of Revelation, certainly among the most challenging in the Bible. But the principle of duodirectionality opens a window into the author's own understanding of this complex vision. Whatever else they may mean, the trumpets are clearly a response to the prayers of the saints for justice in relation to the persecutions that have taken place during the course of

Christian history. In the seven trumpets God acknowledges the cry of the souls under the altar by sending judgments down on their enemies. We have, therefore, learned something very important about the trumpets. We must not interpret them primarily as natural disasters or random events, but as focused judgments on the wicked. They are God's way of assuring the saints that He is still in control of our world, even when things seem totally in chaos.

The principle of duodirectionality, then, is a marvelous tool to open up some of the deep things of Revelation. It gives the reader a window into the purpose and understanding of the author, whether one thinks of the author as the human being named John or as the divine source of the visions, Jesus.

Chiastic Structure

> ### The Principle of Duodirectionality
> "The key to the author's intention for difficult passages in Revelation is often located in a preceding statement, usually at the climax of the preceding section of the book."
>
> 1. Give careful attention to the "seams" of Revelation (passages at the transition point between major visions).
>
>   Examples:
>   - Rev. 1:19
>   - Rev. 3:21
>   - Rev. 6:9, 10
>   - Rev. 11:18
>   - Rev. 12:17
>   - Rev. 15:1-4
>   - Rev. 17:1-6
>   - Rev. 21:1-8
>
> 2. Notice words, phrases, and ideas that recall the previous vision or section.
> 3. Notice words, phrases, and ideas that anticipate the next vision or section.
> 4. Determine the theological impact of number 3.

A third major literary strategy of the author of Revelation seems to be structuring the book into a chiasm. If you've never heard it before "chiasm" sounds like a fancy word you shouldn't have to know. Actually the word is based on the Greek letter "X," which is pronounced "kai" (a hard "ch" sound). Chiasm describes a way of thinking and writing that was quite typical of Hebrew people but is foreign to us today. For example, a typical outline today moves from A to B to C. In a chiastic outline, however, things happen differently. You go from A to B and back to A. But the second "A" is enhanced, sort of like a musical scale. In a musical scale you keep coming back to the same keys but at a higher pitch.

Unlike Western thinking, which moves forward to a conclusion that is usually quite different than the starting point, in chiastic thinking you make a full circle and return to where you started. It is a different kind of logic, another form of reasoning. The "X" (chi) is a good illustration because you move from the A point to the center ("B") and back to an A point at the

---

Chiastic Parallels in Revelation

Prologue and Epilogue

1:1	"things which must happen soon"	22:6
1:3	"blessed is the one who keeps . . ."	22:7
1:3	"the time is near"	22:10
1:4	"the seven churches"	22:16

Seven Churches and New Jerusalem

1:17	"first and last"	21:6
2:7	"tree of life"	22:2
2:11	"second death"	21:8
3:12	"New Jerusalem"	21:10

The Seals and the Consummation

4:4	"24 elders"	19:4
4:6	"four living creatures"	19:4
5:6; 7:17	"the Lamb"	19:7, 9
6:2	rider on white horse	19:11
6:8	"sword"	19:15, 21

Church Militant   **Church Triumphant**

---

end. The words and ideas at the beginning parallel the words and ideas at the end. The second part echoes to the second from the end, and the third part the third from the end, etc., until you reach the center. Now in Greek logic—the ABC approach—the climax occurs at the end. But in Hebrew logic—the ABA approach—the climax comes at the center. Having made the main point, the author goes back to review how he or she got there, helping the reader to tie things up into a comfortable package.

What might make us suspect that the author constructed the book of Revelation as a giant chiasm? My Revelation teacher at Andrews University back in the 1970s, Kenneth Strand, is the one who first noticed the chiastic structure of the book of Revelation. He started by looking at the Prologue, the first eight verses of the book, and comparing it with the Epilogue, the last 15 or so. Notice the following list of "Chiastic parallels" as a starting point for verifying Strand's observations. Because the parallels are far more extensive in the text itself, the examples are only selective.

The Prologue and the Epilogue

Notice first the list of parallel texts under *"Prologue and Epilogue."* Here you find Revelation 1:1 and Revelation 22:6 reflecting each other.

"The revelation of Jesus Christ, which God gave him to show his servants *what must soon take place.* He made it known by sending his angel to his servant John" (Rev. 1:1, NIV).

"The angel said to me, 'These words are trustworthy and true. The Lord, the God of the spirits of the prophets, sent his angel to show his servants *the things that must soon take place'"* (Rev. 22:6, NIV).

While the translation of the italicized words differs slightly, the original Greek of both texts uses the exact same wording. Both the beginning and the end of the book of Revelation mention "the things that must soon take place." It is but one of nearly a dozen striking parallels of word and phrase between the Prologue and the Epilogue of Revelation. Note how Revelation 1:3 echoes Revelation 22:7, 10:

"Blessed is the one who reads *the words of this prophecy,* and blessed are those who hear it and take to heart what is written in it, because *the time is near"* (Rev. 1:3, NIV).

" 'Behold, I am coming soon! *Blessed is he who keeps the words of the prophecy* in this book.' . . . Then he told me, 'Do not seal up *the words of the prophecy* of this book, because *the time is near.'"* (Rev. 22:7-10, NIV).

Needless to say, still other parallels occur between Revelation 1:3 and

Revelation 22:7-10. A careful study of the Prologue and the Epilogue shows a consistent and intentional symmetry between them.

The Seven Churches and the New Jerusalem

A similar situation exists when you compare the letters to the seven churches with the New Jerusalem section of the book. The contents of the second part of Revelation match that of the next to last part. For example, in Revelation 2:7 Jesus promises the overcomer in Ephesus the right to the tree of life, which is in the paradise of God. Revelation 22:2 describes the tree of life in the New Jerusalem, now available to the redeemed. Similarly, Revelation 2:11 assures the overcomers that the second death will not hurt them, Revelation 20:14 and 21:8 describe death being thrown into the lake of fire, and Revelation 21:4 announces that God will wipe every tear from their eyes because there will be no more death in the New Jerusalem. Strand has pointed more than a dozen major parallels between the seven letters and the new earth portion of Revelation.

In the verses just mentioned we have the basis for another observation by Strand. You will notice that in the letters to the seven churches the things Jesus promises become actual reality in the context of the New Jerusalem. This led Strand to conclude that the first part of the Revelation chiasm relates to the big picture of earth's history running from the author's day to the Second Coming. The second half of Revelation, on the other hand, deals with the final events of earth's history.

We have already taken a look at the parallel between the trumpets and the bowls and will examine below the "B" parallel between the seals and Revelation 19, 20. The center of the chiasm ("D"), which turns out to be chapters 12-14 (here I differ a little with Strand), is the climax, the key to the whole puzzle. At the center of the book of Revelation looms the great final battle between the dragon and the remnant. This section, with its messages from three angels, is what the whole structure works toward and away from. It is the key to understanding the whole book. And the center of the center is the three angels' messages (Rev. 14:6-12). Here God sets forth His agenda for the final events of earth's history.

So Revelation, as a whole, functions as a giant chiasm made up of seven major parts with a prologue and an epilogue. I illustrate the big picture of this outline in the following box. The full outline of the book appears at the end of this chapter.

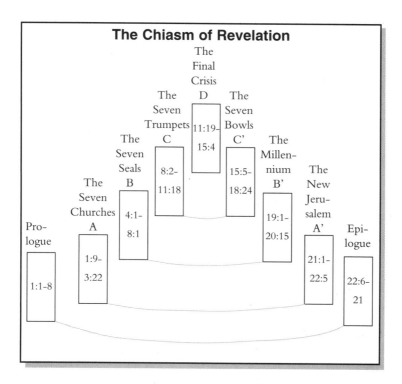

The Chiasm of Revelation

The Seals and Revelation 19–20

Before we close our brief exploration of Revelation's chiasm, I would like to demonstrate how helpful Strand's chiastic structure can be. We will compare the seals (chapters 4, 5, 6, and 7) with Revelation 19, the chiastic counterpart of the seals. Refer back to the part of the earlier chart titled "The Seals and the Consummation." A comparison of chapters 4 and 5 with chapter 19 is interesting. Both are similar as worship scenes. In fact, the only places in Revelation where you have elders, four living creatures, the throne, and scenes of praise and worship are in the seals and Revelation 19. So the material is strongly parallel. But notice also the interesting difference: Why does God receive praise in chapters 4 and 5? In chapter 4 God gets praised for being the Creator and in chapter 5 the Lamb receives praise for His sacrifice on the cross. So Creation and the cross are the grounds for praise in these passages. What is the reason for praise in Revelation 19? The conquest of end-time Babylon.

What does this parallel reveal to us about Revelation 4, 5? It tells us that Revelation 4, 5 is not an end-time passage as many have thought. Instead, the two chapters set the tone for the whole book of Revelation by building on creation and the cross, the foundation of Christian theology. Revelation 4 and 5 occur, therefore, at the beginning of the Christian Era. On the other hand, Revelation 19, in the latter part of the book—the end-time section of the book—celebrates the end-time events and the completion of the destruction of Babylon. Such insights caused Strand to see the first half of the chiasm as chiefly historical and the last half as primarily eschatological or end-time. A careful comparison of Revelation 6:10 with Revelation 19:1-2 confirms this. In the former text souls under the altar cry out, "How long, O Lord, will you be not judging and not avenging?" Then Revelation 19 depicts celebration because God *has* judged and *has* avenged. If you continue your way through Revelation 4-6 and Revelation 19, you will see perhaps a dozen or more examples of these kinds of parallels.

So a major structural aspect of Revelation is the way material at the beginning of the chiasm compares with material at the end. The first half of Revelation focuses on the large sweep of Christian history, with special emphasis on its beginnings with the cross and the exaltation of Jesus to His heavenly role and status. The second half of Revelation concentrates on the final events of earth's history. The first half looks forward to God's great final acts in the controversy, while the second half chronicles the completion of those acts and eventually treats them as if they were already in the past.

The Hebrew Sanctuary in the Book of Revelation

I'd like to turn now to the last major structural strategy of Revelation that we will examine in this chapter. Careful investigation suggests that the Hebrew sanctuary of the Old Testament and its rituals play a major role in the organization of the book of Revelation. A full understanding of Revelation requires knowledge of the Old Testament sanctuary, its furnishings, and the various feasts and sacrifices that occurred there. The major furnishings of the Hebrew sanctuary appear in the chart below along with the chapters in Revelation that mention them.

The Old Testament sanctuary complex was a rectangle made up of two squares. The western square contained the tabernacle (tent) or temple and the eastern square occupied the outer court. At the center of the outer court stood the altar of burnt offering, while at the center of the other square was the ark of the covenant. The tabernacle (tent) was a smaller

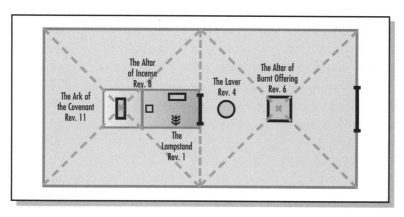

rectangle located in the western square (left). It consisted of a square area (actually a cube, as the height equaled the length and width) called the Most Holy Place, in the center of which rested the ark of the covenant. The holy place filled the rest of the tabernacle, and its shape was the same as the larger compound, a rectangle in "2 x 4" shape. The holy place contained three pieces of furniture: the seven-branched lampstand (to the south of the room), the table of showbread (to the north), and the golden altar of incense (to the west). The remaining major article of furniture was the laver (signified by the circle) in the outer court.

From a New Testament perspective, the sanctuary is rich in Christian symbolism. The furnishings and the activities in the sanctuary all point to the person and work of Jesus Christ (see Hebrews 8-10, for example). The sanctuary itself in the left half of the sanctuary compound represents the heavenly side of God's saving activity, including intercession, judgment, and divine authority. The outer court in the right half represents the earthly aspect of God's saving activity, including Christ's baptism and his death on the cross (Rev. 11:1, 2).

The incarnation of Jesus involved a movement from His position on the heavenly throne (represented by the ark in the Most Holy Place—Rev. 11:19) down to earth (the right half of the sanctuary compound). The center piece of His earthly work was the cross (represented by the altar of burnt offering). At His ascension to heaven Jesus went from right to left in the sanctuary diagram. The sanctuary compound also represents the path people take back to God. The cross (burnt offering altar) attracts people through the gate, they move to baptism (laver), enter the fellowship of heavenly places in the church (Rev. 1:12-20), and through judgment are granted intimate relationship with God for eternity (Rev. 11:18, 19).

As indicated in the above chart, many aspects of the sanctuary find their fulfillment, in one way or another, in the book of Revelation. We will begin our look at the role of the sanctuary in Revelation with an examination of the introductory scenes to the seven major visions in the book.

The Introductory Scenes

The book of Revelation seems to be structured to some degree on the Old Testament sanctuary and its services, feast days, and furniture. As we noted in the chiastic structure above, the book of Revelation has seven major divisions. At the beginning of each is an introductory section that contains recollections of the sanctuary. For example, Revelation 1:12-20, the introduction to the seven letters of Revelation 2 and 3, pictures Jesus among the sanctuary candlesticks. Revelation 8:3-5, the introduction to the trumpets, presents a view of the altar of incense. Throughout the book of Revelation each of the seven-fold visions has an introduction that reminds us of the Old Testament sanctuary or Temple. We will briefly examine each of the sanctuary introductions.

Sanctuary Introductions	
Introduction	**Main Vision**
1. Rev. 1:12-20	1. Seven Churches (Rev. 2; 3)
2. Rev. 4:1–5:14	2. Seven Seals (Rev. 6:1–8:1)
3. Rev. 8:2-6	3. Seven Trumpets (Rev. 8:7–11:18)
4. Rev. 11:19	4. The Wrath of the Nations (Rev. 11:19–15:4)
5. Rev. 15:5-8	5. The Seven Bowls (Rev. 16:1–18:24)
6. Rev. 19:1-10	6. The End of Evil (Rev. 19:11–20:15)
7. Rev. 21:1-8	7. The New Jerusalem (Rev. 21:9–22:5)

Revelation 1:12-20. The introductory vision to the seven churches pictures Jesus Christ among seven golden lampstands (Rev. 1:12-20). This reminds us somewhat of Solomon's Temple which contained 10 golden lampstands in the holy place. Here in Revelation one like a son of man stands in the middle of the lampstands wearing a foot-length robe and a golden sash, garments typical of the high priest. Is this scene located in the heavenly sanctuary or on earth?

Clearly, in this vision Christ is not in the heavenly sanctuary, but on Patmos. John himself was on Patmos at the beginning of the vision (Rev. 1:9). He hears behind him a loud "voice" that sounds like a trumpet (verse 10). When he turns around to "see the voice" he experiences a vision of Christ (verses 12, 13). So this vision is on earth and not in heaven. The lampstands are not pieces of heavenly furniture, but represent the churches on earth (verse 20). And if we still had any doubts, they are dispelled by the discovery that it is not until Revelation 4:1 that John gets called up into heavenly places. So this scene is not a vision of the heavenly sanctuary, rather it uses a sanctuary image to describe what Jesus is doing on earth among the churches.

But in what way is it appropriate for Christians to apply heavenly sanctuary imagery to the church on earth? Matthew 18:20 hints at the answer: "For where two or three come together in my name, there am I with them" (NIV). This is a virtual quotation of a common saying among the rabbis. "Where two sit together to study the Torah, the Shekinah glory rests between them" (Mishnah, Pirke Aboth 3:2). Jesus was alluding to this first-century rabbinical tradition to communicate a powerful message about Himself. He replaces the Shekinah glory with Himself. In His person the glory of the sanctuary is present whenever two or three gather together in His name. So in Matthew 18 Christ's Shekinah presence is in the midst of the church. That is the message of Revelation 1 as well. It is the sanctuary on earth and not the heavenly one that the chapter has in view. Furthermore, it is the sanctuary of the church. And the church is found wherever two or three come together in the name of Jesus.

Revelation 4, 5. In the vision of Revelation 4, 5 we clearly move into the heavenly sanctuary. A voice summons John up through an open door into the heavenly throne room (Rev. 4:1). The passage contains abundant sanctuary imagery—more, in fact, than the rest of the book combined. For example, the three stones mentioned in connection with God's throne (verse 3) all form part of the breastplate of the high priest in the earthly sanctuary (Ex. 28:17-21). The 24 elders bring to mind the 24 courses of priests in the Old Testament sanctuary (1 Chron. 24) The lamps (Rev. 4:5) remind us of the sanctuary lamps of Revelation 1. The four living creatures around the throne (verses 6-8) allude to Solomon's Temple with its two smaller angels on the ark and two larger ones spreading their wings over the ark in the Most Holy Place (1 Kings 6:23-28). This passage also mentions the Lamb that was slain, incense ascending, and a trumpet. So we find a thorough mix of images from the entire sanctuary in Revelation 4 and 5. This raises the question: What aspect of the sanctuary is in view here since we observe images from throughout the sanctuary?

Two occasions in the ancient tabernacle services involved the entire sanctuary. The first consisted of the inauguration of the sanctuary itself. The inauguration service touched every article of furniture and every detail in one way or another. The other occasion was the Day of Atonement. Is it possible to know which event is in view here? Is the reader to see in Revelation 4, 5 the inauguration of the heavenly sanctuary or the Day of Atonement?

A careful look at the evidence suggests the inauguration. Day of Atonement imagery clearly occurs in the second half of the book of Revelation, but the evidence for it here is weak. For example, in the Day of Atonement the special sacrificial animal was the goat. But chapter 5 centers on a lamb instead of a goat. The priests sacrificed lambs during the dedication of the Temple, but not goats (1 Kings 8:63). So the fact that a lamb appears in this vision would suggest a focus on inauguration rather than on the Day of Atonement. We see this confirmed by the fact that whatever is taking place here is in direct response to what happened on the cross. It is the sacrifice that dedicates the temple. Further, we find no reference to judgment in Revelation 4 and 5, which we would expect if the Day of Atonement were in view. Instead of judgment, intercession is the focus here, with incense continually going up (Rev. 5:8). So the scene of Revelation 4 and 5 would appear to be a symbolic description of the inauguration of the sanctuary in heaven.

Revelation 8:3-5. Since this passage is quite a bit shorter than the previous one, we will quote it here:

"Another angel, who had a *golden censer,* came and stood at the *altar.* He was given much *incense* to offer, with the prayers of all the saints, on the *golden altar* before the throne. . . . Then the angel took the *censer,* filled it with fire from the altar, and hurled it on the earth; and there came peals of thunder, rumblings, flashes of lightning, and an earthquake" (Rev. 8:3-5, NIV).

Here we see three sanctuary images: golden incense altar, incense, and the censer. It seems clear from them that the focus of this particular introduction is on intercession. In the sanctuary God intercedes for His people. The prayers of the saints combine with the incense to enhance their effectiveness before God.

Revelation 11:19. At the very center of the book and its sanctuary introductions comes Revelation 11:19: "Then God's *temple* in heaven was opened, and within his *temple* was seen the *ark of his covenant.* And there came flashes of lightning, rumblings, peals of thunder, an earthquake and a great hailstorm" (NIV). In moving from Revelation 8 to Revelation 11 we shift from the holy place of the sanctuary to the Most Holy Place, the site of the ark of the covenant. The word for "temple" here is the Greek term *naos.* It is a special term reserved especially for the Most Holy Place of the Temple. This was true not only in the Bible, but also of the ancient Greek temples one can still see in Egypt today. When the tour guide brings you to the inner shrine of a temple he will announce, "This is the *naos,* the holiest part of the temple." So this passage has a clear focus on the ark and the Most Holy Place. Verse 18 also mentions the final judgment:

"The nations were angry; and your wrath has come. *The time has come for judging the dead,* and for rewarding your servants the prophets and your saints and those who reverence your name, both small and great—and for destroying those who destroy the earth" (Rev. 11:18, NIV).

Revelation 11:18 is the first verse in Revelation that describes judgment as a present reality (in Revelation 6:10 it has not yet begun). In the context of that judgment we view the ark in the Most Holy Place. So I would conclude that Revelation 11:19 contains the theme of judgment just as Revelation 8 implied the theme of intercession.

Revelation 15:5-8. The next sanctuary introduction appears in Revelation 15:5-8:

"After this I looked and in heaven *the temple, that is, the tabernacle of the Testimony,* was opened. Out of the temple came the seven angels with the seven plagues. They were *dressed in clean, shining linen and wore golden sashes around their chests.* Then one of the four living creatures gave to the seven angels seven *golden bowls* filled with the wrath of God, who lives for ever and ever. And *the temple was filled with smoke* from the glory of God and from his power, and *no one could enter the temple* until the seven plagues of the seven angels were completed" (Rev. 15:5-8, NIV).

This passage contains a large number of sanctuary images. We have already mentioned the term *naos,* the Greek word for the Most Holy Place of the Temple. It occurs again here, translated "temple." The angels in the scene wear white and gold garments, reminding us of those worn by the priests. The phrase "tabernacle of the testimony" occurs in Numbers 17 and to the Most Holy Place there. But perhaps the primary background to this introduction is imagery that we find in Exodus 40 and 1 Kings 8, the accounts of the dedications of the tabernacle and the Temple, respectively.

Revelation 15:5-8, therefore, incorporates imagery related to the inauguration of the Old Testament sanctuary. But we notice a difference here. In Revelation 15 and 16 the temple is emptied and never put back in use again. The powerful message seems to be that the temple in heaven is abandoned and intercession is no longer available. Inaugurated in Revelation 4 and 5, the sanctuary then went through phases of intercession and judgment, and is here shut down, the services ceasing.

Revelation 19:1-10. The scene in Revelation 19:1-10 has many remarkable parallels to Revelation 5. Portraying celebration and praise, it mentions worship, the throne, the Lamb, and the 24 elders, among other things. So it is the chiastic counterpart of the worship scene in Revelation 4 and 5. But we notice a most interesting difference, however. It has a total absence of explicit sanctuary images: there is no incense, no altar, no ark of the covenant, no doors or any other article of furniture from the Old Testament tabernacle. Worship is taking place, just as it does in Revelation 5, but all direct reference to the sanctuary and its furnishings is absent.

Revelation 21:1-8. The final sanctuary introduction in Revelation occurs in chapter 21, verses 1-8. Verses 2 and 3 contain a remarkable statement:

"I saw the Holy City, *the new Jerusalem, coming down out of heaven from God,* prepared as a bride beautifully dressed for her husband. And I heard a loud voice from the throne, saying, 'Now *the dwelling of God is with men,* and he will live with them. They will be his people, and God himself will be with them and be their God'" (NIV).

Where is the sanctuary in this text? The original for "dwelling" (verse 3) is actually "tabernacle" or tent. God's tabernacle (same word as in Rev. 15:5-8) has come down to earth. But verse 2 makes it clear that this "tabernacle" is actually the New Jerusalem, the holy city itself. So in Revelation 21, 22, the New Jerusalem becomes the sanctuary. It has the shape of a cube, just like the Most Holy Place of the sanctuary. In fact the only perfect cubes in the Bible are the Most Holy Place and the New Jerusalem. This perfect cube has as its foundation the stones that are in the high priest's breastplate. So the New Jerusalem, in essence, becomes the Most Holy Place. God and the Lamb themselves become the temple of the city.

That temple also has sacrificial services. "No longer will there be any curse. The throne of God and of the Lamb will be in the city, and his *servants* will serve him" (Rev. 22:3, NIV). The word "servants" reflects a Greek word that is not the usual one for servant or slave. Instead it has to do with priestly, even sacrificial, service in the sanctuary. They will serve Him in the city that has become the eschatological temple.

In conclusion, we see that each of the seven visionary introductions in the book of Revelation have a theme related to the sanctuary. The accompanying box lists the themes.

The Meaning of the Sanctuary Introductions	
Introduction	**Meaning**
1. Rev. 1:12-20	1. Church = Temple
2. Rev. 4:1–5:14	2. Inauguration
3. Rev. 8:2-6	3. Intercession
4. Rev. 11:19	4. Judgment
5. Rev. 15:5-8	5. De-Inauguration
6. Rev. 19:1-10	6. Absence
7. Rev. 21:1-8	7. City = Temple

As we examine these themes as a whole, it becomes apparent that we have a complete cycle moving from the earthly temple in chapter 1 (the seven churches) to the earthly temple in chapters 21 and 22 (the New Jerusalem). On the next chart below we can observe an earth-heaven-earth pattern. When the New Jerusalem comes down out of heaven, the heavenly sanctuary returns to earth (Rev. 21:2, 3). The New Jerusalem on earth is the chiastic counterpart to the scene of Jesus among the lampstands in chapter 1. In both cases the scene takes place on earth. But scenes 2-6— the five sanctuary introductions in the middle of the book—all occur in heaven and are related to the heavenly sanctuary.

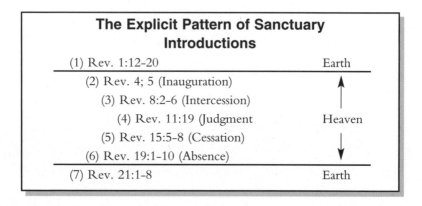

The Explicit Pattern of Sanctuary Introductions	
(1) Rev. 1:12-20	Earth
(2) Rev. 4; 5 (Inauguration)	
(3) Rev. 8:2-6 (Intercession)	
(4) Rev. 11:19 (Judgment	Heaven
(5) Rev. 15:5-8 (Cessation)	
(6) Rev. 19:1-10 (Absence)	
(7) Rev. 21:1-8	Earth

Here's the point I want you to notice in particular: Taken together, *sanctuary introductions 2 through 6 present a complete history of the heavenly sanctuary throughout the Christian Era.* The sanctuary begins its function with an inauguration ceremony. That history continues with a phase of intercession, followed by judgment, abandonment, and eventually absence. During the Christian Era God establishes the sanctuary, it goes through its phases of intercession and judgment, then closes its work and is no longer needed in the New Jerusalem. So the sanctuary introductions of Revelation provide a beautiful picture of the role of the heavenly sanctuary throughout the Christian Era of earth's history.

It is interesting how much of the book of Revelation depends on the sanctuary and how the sanctuary even helps to structure the book. The sanctuary imagery of the book of Revelation seems to be purposefully chosen rather than randomly placed.

Conclusion

The book of Revelation is challenging and difficult, but its deep things begin to open up when we apply the author's own strategies to gain an insight into the book's meaning and purpose. So with regard to structure, careful attention to detail in Revelation helps one unpack the book and see things that we would otherwise miss. The structure of Revelation contains many clues by which the author has sought to reveal his meaning. As we observe these special features of Revelation, we gain a clearer understanding of what is happening in the book.

In the next chapter we will turn to another major key to discovering the deep things of God in this book: the way the author alludes to the Old Testament and builds on its symbolism. Discovering the Old Testament background to passages in Revelation opens up a whole new dimension of understanding.

7

RECLAIMING THE PAST: OLD TESTAMENT ALLUSIONS AND THEIR SIGNIFICANCE

The year was 1984, a date made ominous by the novelist George Orwell. But for me several positive events marked the year, including moving into the home we still live in and being hired to teach at the seminary, where I still remain. But perhaps the most unforgettable moment of that year occurred during one of the debates that led up to the election that returned Ronald Reagan to the office of the United States presidency.

The race for the nomination of the Democratic Party was chiefly between Walter Mondale and Gary Hart. Gary Hart would later become infamous for his dalliances with women other than his wife. But at the time of this particular debate, he was actually the leading candidate for the nomination, and his opponent was considering desperate measures to turn the tide. No one could have anticipated that the entire nomination process would turn on a simple phrase.

In the course of the debate Gary Hart talked about his vision for improving the country. Walter Mondale received a moment for rebuttal. He said that his opponent had a lot of things to say, but that the really decisive issue was "Where's the beef?" At first blush it would seem that Mondale thought the agriculture vote would turn the tide in his favor. But actually his comment had nothing to do with the meat raising and packing industry.

You see, just before this debate a major hamburger chain began airing a charming TV ad that mocked the size of the portions at its major rival. A "little old lady" sat at the table of the rival chain and someone placed a hamburger in front of her. The bun was generous in its proportions, promising a sizable meal. But when the woman lifted off the top half of the bun, all you could see was a tiny little piece of meat, not much wider than a quarter. Looking with stunned surprise, she said with the quavering voice of the aged, "Where's the beef?" The campaign was a smash success. All over the country people were reciting the lines from the TV commercial. The woman became a star overnight at the age of 85.

What was the message of the commercial? It didn't matter what kind of claims the other chain made for its hamburger sandwich. What counted was the meal that one actually received. The TV ads challenged the viewer to compare the offerings of the rival chains and discover the benefits of changing one's eating destination. By invoking the phrase from the burger commercial, Mondale adroitly raised the question of whether Hart's promises contained substance or mere words.

With this phrase Mondale communicated much more than a message about American agriculture. By a simple allusion to the TV commercial he called his opponent's credibility into question. Perceptions of his opponent changed overnight, even though Mondale himself had delivered little "beef" to promote that change. With a simple phrase the candidate succeeded in turning his opponent into a national laughingstock, even before the latter's marital indiscretions became public knowledge and forever ruined his political career. Such is the power of a simple phrase. What may not be quite so obvious are the implications this story has for our study of the book of Revelation. That will become apparent in the next few pages.

The Importance of the Old Testament in Revelation

If you have ever read the Old Testament or even a collection of children's stories based on the Old Testament, it won't take you long to figure out the importance of the Old Testament for the message of Revelation. William Milligan, a leading commentator on the book of Revelation about 100 years ago, was so impressed with this point that he made the following statement:

"The book of Revelation is absolutely steeped in the memories, the incidents, the thought, and the language of the church's past. To such an extent is this the case that *it may be doubted whether it contains a single figure not drawn from the Old Testament,* or a single complete sentence not more or less built up of materials brought from the same source."

So if you were to study the book of Revelation without reference to the Old Testament, the genuine meaning of the book would largely remain a mystery to you. It could be argued, as Milligan does, that virtually every word, phrase, and idea finds its source somewhere in the Old Testament. And Milligan is not alone in his opinion. More recently a major commentator in the German language, Heinrich Kraft, said the following (translated from German):

· "We can say, in a general way, that until we have succeeded in laying out the Old Testament source for an apocalyptic prophecy, we have not interpreted that passage."

So I think it's very clear that if we don't understand the Old Testament, we are not going to comprehend the book of Revelation either. The book contains about 2,000 references of one kind or another to the Old Testament. It means that the study of Revelation ties us to the Old Testament in many, many ways. You could even say that the Old Testament is "the key to the code" in which John wrote the book of Revelation. By my estimation, 80 to 85 percent of the hundreds of symbols in the book of Revelation are best understood by reference to the Old Testament.

But we face a serious problem here. Most of these "references" to the Old Testament are simply a word, a phrase, often just the barest hint of a connection. This allusive use of the Old Testament leaves a lot of room for question and speculation. Without careful study and comparison, it is easy to misinterpret the Revelator's utilization of the Old Testament. So we need to chart a path toward understanding the deeper issues in the author's relationship to the Hebrew Scriptures.

Types of Usage

In general there seem to be four basic ways that New Testament writers reflect on and employ the Old Testament. We can describe each of the four ways with one word: citation, quotation, allusion, and echo. Let's define the terms briefly and then see how they apply to the book of Revelation.

Citation

The first type of usage is called "citation." Citation takes place when a person quotes another piece of literature fairly extensively and then tells you where you can find the quotation. A good example of this in today's world is the use of footnotes in scholarly literature. You quote something you have read and then give the reference so that everyone knows where you got it. Citation is the easiest way to spot references to earlier material because the author is clear about what is being quoted and where it came from.

Quotation

A "quotation" is very similar to a citation in the sense that it involves a significant body of quoted material. The difference in this case is the lack of a "footnote." The author doesn't tell you where the quote came from and just assumes that you will recognize it. The material contains enough words in a row that an educated reader or one who knows the author personally would have no question where it came from, even without a reference. For example: "Oh, say, can you see, by the dawn's early light, what so proudly we hailed, at the twilight's last gleaming?" Nearly every American immediately recognizes the opening words of the national anthem of the United States. The mere reading of the words sets off a tune in my mind. With a quotation like this it is not difficult to determine the source, if you are at all familiar with it.

Allusion

The third way New Testament writers employed the Old Testament is called "allusion." To allude to previous literature is much more mysterious than citation or quotation. An allusion is also a serious attempt to point readers to a commonly-recognized source, but the reference may be limited to just a word, a phrase, or an idea. With allusion the reader must fill in the blanks. Allusions to the Old Testament in Revelation are more challenging than citations or quotations because it is difficult to discover where the author is heading, particularly after 1,900 years have gone by. Because the author intends the reader to pick up on the connection with the Old Testament, some scholars prefer the term "direct allusion" to label that intention.

Echo

The fourth way that the Old Testament is used by New Testament writers goes by the word "echo." Echoes are similar to allusions in that they involve merely a word, a phrase, or an idea from the Old Testament. But there is one major difference. As has been said, a direct allusion is a serious attempt to point readers to a commonly recognized source, but with an echo the author has no intention to direct readers to a specific source, literary or otherwise. A writer can "echo" the language of previous literature without being aware of it. The language comes to the writer "in the air" of the world he or she lives in. The reader is expected to understand the meaning of the term, but not to tie it to any particular literary predecessor.

An Important Distinction

The frustrating thing about the book of Revelation is that it never cites or quotes the Old Testament. If it did, our task would be easier. But at no point in the book do we find such a lengthy use of the Old Testament that we could know without a shadow of a doubt exactly where that quotation came from. The nearest thing to a citation is in Revelation 15, which introduces the Song of Moses by the sea. Scholars immediately recognize that as a reference to Exodus 15. But if you compare Revelation 15 with Exodus 15, you discover that John is not quoting the Song of Moses. Instead, he draws the words of the song in Revelation 15 from a collage of eight or nine Old Testament passages, none of them from the book of Exodus. So the "song of Moses" in chapter 15 is not a true citation of the Old Testament. The book of Revelation never cites or quotes the Old Testament. It requires that the reader either recognize the references from previous experience or do enough background work to discover them.

Most of John's readers would probably have immediately caught his allusions to the Old Testament. They were familiar with John, his teaching, and the Old Testament. After years of relationship they would be ready to pick up on the hints that he dropped here and there. But today, we can easily miss the allusions, and in the process the message of the book becomes distorted. But overlooking messages is not the only possible problem. Overeager interpreters may find allusions that John or Jesus never intended! Sometimes John alludes to the Old Testament, hoping the reader will recognize the source and consider its meaning for what he is saying. At other times John merely echoes Old Testament language and does not intend to refer to the Hebrew Scriptures. Distinguishing between the two is extremely important.

The Function of Allusions

The purpose of an allusion is to lead the reader to consider a specific passage of the Old Testament and apply its significance to the passage of Revelation in question. John intends the reader to recognize the allusion and be aware of its larger context. That context, in a sense, becomes an extended context for Revelation itself. A word, a phrase, or a symbol can become a picture that replaces a thousand words. As you read Revelation you need to do it in the light of Old Testament passages that are alluded to in their context. Recognizing a direct allusion opens fresh windows into the author's meaning. Missing the allusion leaves the author's intention in doubt.

The Mondale story at the beginning of the chapter illustrates the process well. In using the phrase "Where's the beef?" Mondale was counting on the debate's audience to be aware not only of the phrase but of the whole context of the burger commercial. Many who missed the reference, for whatever reason, turned to their neighbor and said, "What's everybody laughing about?" They needed an explanation. Picking up on the larger background context was crucial to a correct understanding of Mondale's point.

The Function of Echos

An echo, on the other hand, is not based on conscious intention. John may use the language of the Old Testament without being consciously aware of where it came from. An echo is a usage that is "in the air," something people just pick up from the environment in which they live. It would be particularly easy to echo the Old Testament if you grew up in a Jewish synagogue where you constantly heard the Old Testament quoted and referred to in various ways. It would be natural for you to use language from the Old Testament but you would not always be consciously aware that the Old Testament was the source of the expressions you were using.

How Echos Work

Let me give you an illustration of how echoes work: What is a lemon? Well, it certainly is a citrus fruit with a fairly sour taste. But the term has an extended meaning in American culture. A lemon is a new car that doesn't deliver on its promise. While it may be brand-new, it is dysfunctional, not reliably doing all the things it is supposed to do. It is a shiny new transport device that doesn't deliver the "beef" (sorry!). As a result a lemon gives its owner far too many troubles and spends much too much time in the repair shop.

Now, if you live in the United States, you are familiar with this symbolic use of "lemon." In the context of automobiles, a lemon is a bad car, and the term has been around since the early 1900s. But the popularity of "lemon" increased tremendously when Ralph Nader in 1970 published a book entitled *What to Do With Your Bad Car*. The cover of the book was white and had a picture of a lemon with four plastic wheels on it. Reading the title and then seeing the photo had immediate impact. "Lemon" as a symbol with automotive meaning took off.

But most Americans don't need to know that specific piece of history to understand the extended meaning of "lemon." You pick up that piece of information "in the air" of American culture. And if you are writing or talking about lemons, your audience would automatically understand, whether or not they have ever heard of Ralph Nader. But let's suppose 2,000 years have gone by and the human race has forgotten American civilization. Suddenly someone discovers in a futuristic garbage pile a book you wrote, reads it, and sees a symbolic usage of the word "lemon." What are they going to conclude? If they think "citrus fruit," they will totally miss your point. But if they then dig up Ralph Nader's book, they would understand your book better. They would realize that you are talking about a bad car, not a citrus fruit or something else.

John often echoes the language of the Old Testament. He may not be aware at such times that he is even using it. Nor is he pointing the reader to a specific Old Testament text. But the meaning of the term still occurs in the Old Testament, and we need to go back and dig out the meaning of those echoes. We will understand the echo by studying the Old Testament, but we should not import the larger context of any Old Testament passage in which the "echo word" occurs. The Old Testament context in which an echo appears does not affect the meaning of the text in Revelation.

Decoding Allusions

Here is the crucial issue. How do you know when John is intentionally alluding to the Old Testament, drawing a particular passage into his description of the vision he saw? What evidence do you look for? The process of detecting an allusion is about determining probabilities. The only way I could be absolutely sure exactly what Old Testament background John had in mind would be to ask him myself. But I don't have that option so all I have to go on are the writings that he left behind. But while at times we will be far from certain, with a little effort we can gain a reasonable sense of John's intention. All we have to do is gather the evidence in the text. Let me show you how. But before I do, I need to offer one caveat.

It is crucial that you not just read about this process, but that you try it out yourself in order to master it. You see, I have learned working with students that if I give the following method and do nothing more it doesn't have a long-term effect. So I ask them to do an assignment that requires them to dig deep into a passage of Revelation to determine where the allusions are. If they will examine the evidence of their passage for, say, 20 to 40 hours, things fall into place in spectacular fashion. The day comes when they come to class with shining eyes and a smile saying, "I've got it! It really works! This is the first time in my life I learned directly from the Bible!"

You see most people, even ministers, tend to learn more from books about the Bible than from direct study of Scripture itself. The following method, while somewhat difficult at first, helps people interact with the Bible text in a way that opens its meaning in surprising ways. And after a certain amount of practice detecting allusions, you become more and more adept at recognizing how the book of Revelation uses the Old Testament. After 30 or 40 hours of practice, the book of Revelation seems full of waving arms saying, "I'm from Genesis! I'm from Exodus! I'm from Isaiah!" When this happens Revelation becomes an entirely new book filled with meaning that it did not have before. Here's what you have to do.

Collecting Potential Parallels

The first step in the method is to collect potential parallels to the text in Revelation that you are studying. You can do this in several ways. One is to look at the references printed in Bible margins. Many Bibles contain lists of parallel texts along the side or center margin or sometimes at the bottom of the page. Another source of potential parallels is commentaries on Revelation. Authors of commentaries will often suggest Old Testament texts that they think lie behind the passage in Revelation. Concordances, both print and computer variety, offer a means of collecting possible allusions to the Old Testament in Revelation. You can also find parallels with a computer using the search features of a Bible program. When it comes to margins or commentaries, you certainly don't want to take any of these sources as "gospel." You will want to examine each passage for evidence of John's intention or lack of it.

How do you do that? First of all, it is a good idea to make copies of the passage in Revelation that you are studying and the various texts of the Old Testament that may be parallel to it. That way you can underline, highlight, and make notes right on the pages. Lay the passage in Revelation side by side with each potential Old Testament allusion. Then look for verbal, thematic, and structural parallels.

Verbal Parallels

First of all, search for verbal parallels. You suspect, for example, that Revelation 9:1-6 may be based on Genesis 19. So you make photocopies of both pages out of your Bible in as large a print size as you can and lay the two passages side by side. Read them both carefully and mark every major word that appears in both. What do I mean by major words? Well, they include pretty much everything but "the," "and," "but," and similar words. Such common words have little significance for a parallel. But major words are distinctive enough that their use cries out for the interpreter's attention. Verbal parallels occur wherever you have at least two major words in common between the two texts. Why two? For practical reasons. If you tried to follow up on all the single word parallels in the Bible you would never finish studying a single chapter of Revelation, much less the whole book. Limiting yourself to parallels of two or more words romoves 95 percent of the effort without any significant loss of accuracy.

Let's follow up on that example. In Genesis 19 three strangers visited Abraham. He eventually discovers that one of the strangers is the Lord Himself. The other two, angels, go on to investigate Sodom, a neighboring city renowned for its debauchery and violence. Knowing that he has a nephew there, Abraham pleads with the Lord not to destroy the city and even succeeds in extracting some concessions. But Sodom perishes anyway, and when Abraham gets up the next morning to see what has happened, he sees the smoke of Sodom rising up "like the smoke of a great furnace" (Gen. 19:28). But that is not the last time in the Bible that you can see the same phrase: "When he opened the Abyss, smoke rose from it *like the smoke of a gigantic furnace*" (Rev. 9:2).

Revelation 9:2 contains a verbal parallel to Genesis 19:28. We observe three major words in common between the two texts: "smoke," "great," and "furnace." Does that mean that John was definitely alluding to Genesis 19 in Revelation 9? Not necessarily. Verbal parallels are just part of the evidence you use to determine whether the author is making an intentional allusion or not. Verbal parallels are, however, strong evidence. The more words you have in common between two texts, the more likely it is that one author is quoting another. In fact, if your verbal parallel is extensive—15-20 words in a row—you should probably not speak of an allusion, but rather of a quotation. That level of certainty, however, rarely occurs in Revelation, if at all.

So in the process of comparing texts you begin by noting all the verbal parallels between the texts. Using a pen or a highlighter mark all the major words that appear in both texts. Make note of all verbal parallels such as "smoke of a great furnace," which is probably a highly significant parallel. Verbal parallels form a major part of the evidence base for determining when John is alluding to a particular Old Testament text.

Detecting Verbal Parallels

1. Collect potential parallel texts.
   - ✔ Bible margins
   - ✔ Commentaries
   - ✔ Concordances
   - ✔ Computer Bible programs
2. Copy the passage in Revelation and the potential parallels texts in large print.
3. Using a colored pen or highlighter mark all significant parallel words.

Thematic Parallels

A second piece of evidence to look for is thematic parallels. Thematic parallels can occur in connection with verbal parallels, but you can still have one without verbal parallels. You look for common themes, subjects, and ideas, whether or not the two passages use the same words. In themselves thematic parallels are very weak. When an author has an earlier text in mind, he will normally echo its language as well as its themes. But sometimes the allusion acts like a secret code, as if a nod or a wink were passing between author and reader. At such times an author and reader may both recognize a common theme even though only one word, or sometimes none at all, betray a common element between two texts.

Thematic parallels, therefore, can be difficult to detect. The interpreter comes to the potential parallel text from a knowledge of the book of Revelation, the Old Testament, and a sense of the way John works with the Old Testament. As your experience grows, this difficult process becomes easier and easier. While thematic parallels are weak evidence by themselves, in combination with verbal and structural parallels, the presence of a thematic parallel increases the likelihood that one passage alludes to another.

Perhaps the best way to teach this process is through an example or two. Ezekiel 9:1-7 presents a visionary description, one of the most terrifying in the whole Bible. The prophet sees six men of frightful bearing approaching Jerusalem with weapons in their hands. Among them is a seventh man with a writer's inkhorn at his side. As the seven men enter the Temple of Jerusalem, the glory of God rises up from its place over the ark (in the Most Holy Place) and moves to the door of the Temple. The Lord commands the man with the inkhorn to go from person to person throughout the city and place a mark on the forehead of all those who share God's attitude toward the "abominations" happening in the city and in the Temple.

The man with the inkhorn proceeds from person to person, studies each face, and then either marks the forehead or doesn't. It is a terrifying picture of judgment. No doubt each person holds their breath as the seventh man approaches, because if he places no mark on the forehead, the six armed men behind him immediately strike that individual dead. It is a massacre of all those who don't receive the mark. The result is that the slain fill the Temple and the city and the prophet falls on his face in agony at the scene (Eze. 9:8). Ezekiel learns that the carnage is necessary because the land is full of violence, abuse, and perversion (verse 9). But the judgment also includes mercy. It spares those who "sigh and cry" over the wickedness in the land. So a major theme of the passage in Ezekiel 9 is a mark on peoples' foreheads that protects them from divine judgment.

In Revelation 9:4 (same numerical reference as the mark in Ezekiel!) we encounter a seal placed on the foreheads of the people who are serving God. It protects them against the locusts and the scorpions in the fifth trumpet. Ezekiel and Revelation use different words for "mark." No verbal parallel exists between the texts (the only word in common is "forehead" and a single word is not a verbal parallel), but there is a thematic parallel. The idea of marking the forehead to protect people from the judgments of God makes an interesting and significant correspondence. It is possible that the author of Revelation 9 had Ezekiel 9 in mind even if the passages have only one word in common. Normally, however, allusions are based on more than just a thematic parallel.

Another example of a thematic parallel appears in Revelation 14:6, 7:

"Then I saw another angel flying in midair, and he had the *eternal gospel* to proclaim to those who live on the earth—to every nation, tribe, language and people. He said in a loud voice, "Fear God and give him glory, because *the hour of his judgment* has come. *Worship him who made* the heavens, the earth, the sea and the springs of water" (NIV).

You will notice three italicized phrases in the passage: "eternal gospel," "the hour of his judgment," and "worship him who made." While there are no verbal parallels between these phrases and the Ten Commandments, the italicized phrases express the three motivations for obedience included in the first table of the commandments. The Ten Commandments open with the theme of salvation: "I am the Lord your God, who brought you out of Egypt, out of the land of slavery" (Ex. 20:2, NIV). God's saving action is the primary reason for obeying all the commandments. The next motivation is the aspect of judgment in the second commandment, "visiting the iniquity" (verse 5). The third is the element of creation: "I made you, therefore keep the Sabbath day holy" (verses 8-11). The triple motivations of salvation, judgment, and creation all occur in the italicized passages of Revelation 14:6, 7.

The process of finding thematic parallels is fairly similar to that of searching for verbal ones. You begin by collecting potential parallel texts from margins, commentaries, and other sources. As you compare the Old Testament texts side by side with the passage of Revelation under study, you need to carefully watch for common themes. Since thematic parallels tend to involve large blocks of text, it is helpful to compare the larger context of the

Revelation passage with the larger context of potential Old Testament allusions to see if some thematic parallels might be lurking under the surface of the bigger story. The better you know both the book of Revelation and the Old Testament, the easier it is to detect genuine thematic parallels.

Structural Parallels

The third type of evidence for allusions is called a structural parallel. A structural parallel to the Old Testament in Revelation occurs when you have a whole series of words and ideas in common. A structural parallel might be limited to a paragraph or two in Revelation, or it can cover large sections of the book. A good example of a structural parallel is that between the fifth trumpet (Rev. 9:1-11) and Joel 2:1-11. Note the many parallel words and themes between the texts: a trumpet blast, darkness, locusts, vegetation, horses, chariots, anguish, and a leader. The author of Revelation seems to be following Joel 2:1-11 verse by verse and point by point.

A number of other significant structural parallels exist in the book of Revelation. For example, Revelation 4 has a strong structural parallel to Ezekiel 1. In a doctoral class I once gave the students both the Greek of Ezekiel 1 (the Septuagint translation of the original Hebrew) and of Revelation 4. They discovered that nearly one-third of Revelation 4 had been drawn from Ezekiel 1. It's a powerful relationship. Other examples of structural parallels include Daniel 7 as a structural parallel behind Revelation 13 and 17; Ezekiel 26 and 27 behind Revelation 18; and Ezekiel 40-48 behind the whole story of the New Jerusalem in Revelation 21, 22. And you might suspect the biggest structural parallel already. The book of Revelation as a whole seems to track pretty closely to the book of Ezekiel.

Structural parallels, however, are not limited to references to specific Old Testament texts. They can also involve repeated references to an overarching idea. The trumpets of Revelation, for example, seem clearly based on the Exodus. But the structural parallel is not simply to the book of Exodus. The trumpets allude repeatedly to the theme of the exodus which also occurs in Leviticus, Numbers, and Deuteronomy, and throughout the rest of the Old Testament as well, including the Psalms and the prophets. The plagues of the trumpets parallel those of the Exodus: water turning to blood; hail and fire falling from heaven; darkness; people and animals dying; etc.

In addition, we find many parallels to the creation theme in the trumpets. The Ten Commandments in principle seem to be a major background concept in Revelation 12-14 (and this parallel is not limited to references to Exodus 20). Much of Revelation 14-19 seems drawn from the fall of Babylon theme of Isaiah 44-47, Jeremiah 50-51, and Daniel 5, among others. When looking for structural parallels one should not, therefore, restrict the search just to parallel texts with verbal and thematic parallels. Broader themes of the Old Testament also find repeated reference in Revelation.

So the book of Revelation clearly has many structural parallels to the Old Testament involving both specific texts and major themes and events. Structural parallels are extremely strong evidence for Old Testament allusions in Revelation. For example, wherever you have a verbal parallel to the Exodus theme in the trumpets, the likelihood of a direct allusion is much higher than it would otherwise be.

Weighing the Evidence

All things considered, the more verbal, thematic, and structural parallels you can find, the more likely it becomes that a particular Old Testament passage was in the author's mind. Structural parallels are generally the most certain because of their clarity, but multiple word parallels are also extremely significant. If you have a verbal parallel of six, seven, or eight words, there is probably a direct allusion there. More than eight words in the same order and you should probably be talking about a quotation rather than an allusion.

One problem you may encounter when assessing possible allusions is what to do when a particular phrase or idea is so widely exhibited in the Old Testament that it could point to 10 or 12 different Old Testament texts. At times like that, it becomes particularly difficult to determine which exact one John had in mind. It is more likely in such circumstances that you are dealing with an echo rather than an allusion. The frequent repetition of certain words or ideas placed them "in the air" of John's consciousness. At such times he probably did not have a particular Old Testament source in mind. On the other hand, if the theme or parallel is limited to just one place in the Old Testament, the likelihood that the author of Revelation thought of it when he wrote correspondingly increases.

I assess potential allusions to the Old Testament into five categories of probability: certain, probable, possible, uncertain, and non-allusions. Let's say that a Bible margin reference suggests an allusion to Daniel 6 in Revelation 6. But when you compare the texts you don't find a single verbal, thematic, or structural parallel. That would be what I call a non-allusion. On the other hand, as with Revelation 4 and Ezekiel 1, if you find one verbal parallel after another, many thematic parallels, and a strong structural parallel or two, you have a certain—or at least a probable, allusion.

Weighing the Evidence

One of the chief tasks of the intrepreter of any passage in Revelation is weighing the level of probability that the author of Revelation had particular Old Testament passages in mind. If the interpreter considers it certain or probable that John had an Old Testament text in mind, that text and its Old Testament context should be considered in the interpretation of the passage in Revelation. If the allusion is only possible, that text and its context can be used as supporting evidence for a conclusion about the text in Revelation, but should not form the primary basis. If the potential allusion is judged uncertain or a nonallusion, it should be ignored for the purposes of interpretation.

Definitions

Certain Allusion	Very strong verbal, thematic, and structural parallels; or virtual quotations (eight to 12 verbal parallels)
Probable Allusion	Strong verbal, thematic, and/or structural parallels; verbal parallels of four to seven words without a structural parallel
Possible Allusion	Some verbal (two or three words) and thematic parallels, but without structural support
Uncertain Allusion	Weak verbal or thematic parallel, without structural support
Nonallusion	No evidence of verbal or thematic parallels

Remember, with allusions, it is imperative to go back and examine the Old Testament context carefully. If you find clear parallels, there is probably something in the context of that Old Testament text that the author of Revelation wants you to keep in mind. If it's only a possible allusion, on the other hand, and you observe some common words but are not exactly sure what John's intentions were, you can use those texts in interpretation, but only as supporting evidence for something that is already clear on more solid grounds. You should not use possible or uncertain allusions as primary evidence in support of any interpretation of the book of Revelation.

What Difference Does It Make?

The things we have covered in this chapter may seem to demand a lot of work. No one is likely to invest that much effort in something unless it results in a big payoff. And there is. Detecting allusions is more than just hard work. It is a lot of fun. Like computer games, the solving of difficult problems is not boring. Once you get into this method, you will discover a great deal of enjoyment in the process. And best of all, this method opens up windows of understanding that no other approach to Revelation can.

The best way to learn how to detect allusions in Revelation is actually to do it. At first the task may seem overwhelmingly difficult, but after 10, 20, or 30 hours of practice, it becomes easier and easier as you get a feel for the way John used the Old Testament. So when I teach ministers the book of Revelation I always ask them to take a passage in the book and follow through with this method for themselves. They often grumble and complain about the process at first (ministers are people too). But then, perhaps halfway through the semester, I begin to see shining faces arrive for class. Students will come up to me and say, "It works! It really works! This is the first time I ever learned directly from the Bible!" And the reward is clearly greater than the effort expended.

Let me illustrate the value in this method by examining a passage or two of considerable interest to most Adventist students of Revelation. We'll start with Revelation 14:7, which seems to be the key text of the central part of the book. Let's compare it to Exodus 20:11:

"For in six days *the Lord made the heavens and the earth, the sea,* and all that is in them, but he rested on the seventh day. Therefore the Lord blessed the Sabbath day and made it holy" (Ex. 20:11, NIV).

"He said in a loud voice, 'Fear God and give him glory, because the hour of his judgment has come. Worship *him who made the heavens, the earth, the sea* and the springs of water'" (Rev. 14:7, NIV).

Notice the large number of verbal parallels between Revelation 14:7 and the fourth commandment: God, made, heavens, earth, and sea. Since "the Lord" and "Him" are not exactly the same, we could call this four and a half words in common between the two passages. In both passages God is the one who was involved in creation and made the heavens, earth, and sea. So you have a strong verbal parallel, enough to consider an allusion possible if not probable. Also we notice thematic parallels in the larger context of each passage: salvation, judgment, and creation (mentioned in more detail above). So we have some strong evidence that the author of Revelation had the fourth commandment in mind when he wrote Revelation 14:7.

There's one problem with that conclusion, however. Psalm 146:6 contains exactly the same parallel words as Exodus 20:11 and Revelation 14:7. In fact, in the Greek language the phrasing of Psalm 146:6 is identical to that of Revelation 14:7. Not only that, Psalm 146 also contains the themes of salvation, judgment, and creation, just as Exodus 20 and Revelation 14 do. Could the author of Revelation be alluding to Psalm 146 instead of Exodus 20:11?

No. There is a major difference between Exodus 20 and Psalm 146 as far as Revelation is concerned. Revelation 12-14 contains a major structural parallel to the commandments of God. The "saints" are those who keep the commandments of God (Rev. 12:17; 14:12). By way of contrast, the sea beast commands worship for himself, contrary to the first commandment (Rev. 13:4, 8; cf. Ex. 20:3). The land beast orders people to worship an image, contrary to the second commandment (Rev. 13:15; cf. Ex. 20:4-6), and so on. This strong structural parallel tips the scales in favor of Exodus 20 as the decisive background of the first angel's message in Revelation 14:7. It indicates a clear intention on the part of the author to bring the fourth commandment to view in the context of God's final call to obedience.

Psalm 146, by way of contrast, does not qualify as a certain or probable allusion because it lacks a structural parallel and because Exodus 20 is a far more likely source of the language. If Revelation 14:7 did allude to Psalm 146 it would be the only place in that part of the book that does so. The larger picture of Psalm 146 is simply not crucial to understanding the book of Revelation. So when an ancient reader who knew the Old Testament read Revelation 14:7, that person would have recognized an allusion to the Sabbath command of Exodus 20, not the similar language of Psalm 146.

This insight powerfully affects the interpretation of Revelation 13 and 14. (You might want to see my book *What the Bible Says About the End-time*.)

Let me share one more example of the difference direct allusions can make to the understanding of Revelation. What is the key theme of Revelation 4 and 5? If you go through the passage carefully you will notice that the word "throne" occurs more than 15 times in just two chapters. It is clearly the center point. Everything that happens does so in relation to the throne. Thus the key theme of Revelation 4 and 5 must have to do with power, authority, and the right to rule. "Who is worthy" to open the scroll and sit on the throne with God? The Lamb that was slain (Rev. 5:1-12).

A second look at Revelation 4 and 5 reveals a number of Old Testament structural parallels in the passage: The vision of God's throne in Ezekiel 1. The Ancient of Days on the throne in Daniel 7. Isaiah's vision of the heavenly sanctuary (Isa. 6). Micaiah's vision of God's heavenly courtroom (1 Kings 22). And the experience of Israel in the neighborhood of Mount Sinai (Ex. 19). All in all, we find five major structural parallels to Revelation 4 and 5.

When you look carefully at these five structural parallels in the passage you discover that they include all the great throne passages of the Old Testament. Read each of the Old Testament passages in the light of Revelation 4 and 5, then ask the question, What do all these Old Testament passages have in common with Revelation? The answer you come to is: "The throne of God." Reference to the throne of God (in Exodus 19 that throne is Mount Sinai itself) is the common denominator that ties all these background texts together. So the main theme of Revelation 4 and 5 will be centered in the throne, the place where the Lamb joins the Father in receiving the adoration of the universe.

Recognizing echoes can have a big payoff as well. One echo in the book of Revelation is the concept of vegetation as a symbol of God's people (Rev. 8:7; 9:4). Revelation repeatedly mentions vegetation but does not define what it means by it. John picks up the Old Testament concept of vegetation as a symbol of the people of God (Ps. 1:3; 52:8; Jer. 2:21; Isa. 5:1-7).

Another echo of the Old Testament in Revelation is the trumpet. One hundred and thirty-four times in the Old Testament trumpets are blown— in worship, in battle, at coronations, etc. Surprisingly, the primary use of trumpets in the Old Testament is not for battle, but in worship and prayer (Num. 10:8–10). To understand the trumpets of Revelation, it is critical to know how people used them in ancient times. And as horrific as the images in the trumpet passages are, worship is an integral part of the vision (Rev. 8:2–6; 11:15–18).

Conclusion

In the next chapter we turn to what is perhaps the most important key to interpreting Revelation. It helps to have a strong Old Testament background when you approach Revelation, but that alone doesn't answer the question of *how* the author employs Old Testament material in the book. John is a Christian writer: when he reads the Old Testament he sees Christ as the center and substance of it all. The gospel makes a huge difference in the way you approach the book of Revelation. In the next chapter we will discover how to read both the Old Testament and the book of Revelation as a Christian.

8

SEEING CHRIST IN THE OLD TESTAMENT

As I write, my wife is driving through the countryside on Interstate 57 in central Illinois. The landscape is extremely flat, mostly farmers' fields and grazing grass, with an occasional stand of trees. It is one of those gray days in mid-March. The scenery has little variety to it. So I was a bit startled an hour or so ago to see what appeared to be a gigantic gray cross barely visible against the gray sky in the distance. My first impression was that it must be some sort of industrial contraption that was only shaped like a cross. But as we drew nearer, it became clear that it was truly a representation of the cross of Jesus Christ, the beams set in diamond-shaped metal, perhaps 80 feet high. We saw no sign or other explanation as to why it was there by the road—it just was.

I wondered if that monument was someone's response to a special intervention of God. Perhaps he or she was drowning in a lake and said, "Lord, if You'll save my life right now, I'll build You the biggest monument in the state!" Or perhaps it was supposed to be the bell tower to a church, but they ran out of money before they could build the church! Be that as it may, that cross is certainly the center piece of that portion of the Illinois landscape.

It is like that with the book of Revelation also. If we are not careful, we might get the impression that the beasts, the vultures, the darkness, the earthquakes, and the hailstones are what the book of Revelation is all about. But they are more like the general landscape of the Illinois prairie. The true center piece of the book of Revelation is not war or catastrophe, oil or the Middle East—it is Jesus Christ and Him crucified. His presence permeates the book even when it does not name Him. To read this book without gaining a clearer picture of Jesus is to miss the key point.

In the book of Revelation the symbols of the Old Testament are transformed because of what Christ has done. We have seen that John built Revelation on the Old Testament background and its major themes. But because of Jesus' earthly life, His death and resurrection, and His ministry in the heavenly sanctuary, those Old Testament themes find fresh and creative meaning. Since Revelation is a New Testament book, it picks up on the New Testament's understanding of the Old Testament themes in the light of the Christ event.

The book of Revelation is "the Revelation of Jesus Christ," not that of Moses, Peter, or Daniel. As you go through the book of Revelation, you will find Christ everywhere. Almost every chapter has a reference to Him in one way or another. Besides the direct use of His name, we observe Him in such symbols as Son of Man, Lamb, and child of the woman. In addition to Christ, we also encounter references to churches and the cross (for example, Rev. 1:5, 6, 11; 5:6; 12:11). All this evidence makes clear that Revelation is a Christian book designed to teach us something about Jesus, life in the church, and the meaning of the cross.

An introductory statement in plain language near the beginning (Rev. 1:5, 6) confirms our general observation of the book. There John addresses the reader with a minimum of symbolism, in language that cannot be misunderstood, as if he wanted to establish without question, right at the beginning, just what his book is about. It is about Jesus Christ, the "faithful martyr" (cross), "the firstborn from the dead" (resurrection), and the "ruler of the kings of the earth" (His ministry in heaven). Jesus is "the one who loves us" (present tense), who "freed us from our sins by His blood" (past tense), and who "made us a kingdom and priests" (past tense—the phrases in quotation marks in the past two sentences are my own translation). Because of what Jesus has done, we are loved, we have been freed from the bondage of sin, and we have been elevated to the highest possible status in Him.

So no matter how strange the language of the book may seem, its basic message is in harmony with the themes, words, and ideas of the New Testament. We must never limit Revelation to messages about world history, politics, or the future. Nor must we ever be satisfied with just a prediction of secular realities. A deeply spiritual book, Revelation unveils

Jesus Christ and calls forth mighty songs of worship and praise. If we have failed to see a message about Christ at any point in this book, we have probably not understood that passage. So a fourth step of interpretation is vital. We cannot stop with basic exegesis of the book, with an examination of its structure, or with reference to the Old Testament. We must also read Revelation within the New Testament context as well. To be honest students of the book, we *must* find out how Jesus Christ is the center and substance of each of its parts, even the seals and the trumpets. And we *must* discover how He transforms the symbols and ideas drawn from the Old Testament. Truly in the book of Revelation "all the books of the Bible meet and end" (*The Acts of the Apostles,* p. 585).

Here we need always to keep a basic insight in mind. The New Testament consistently portrays Christ as the One who fulfilled the whole experience of His Old Testament people. The life, death, and resurrection of Jesus Christ is modeled on the experience of Israel. The author of Revelation is constantly pointing to the New Testament Christ, but he does so in Old Testament language. Based on what we have learned so far, that is exactly what we would expect—*God meets people where they are.* John, as he is writing Revelation, sees the Christ of the New Testament in the Old. This leads to amazing depth when you dig behind the references. Let me give you an example.

The Ruler of God's Creation
"To the angel of the church of Laodicea write: These are the words of the Amen, the faithful and true witness, *the ruler of God's creation*" (Rev. 3:14, NIV).

Let's look more carefully at the phrase "the ruler of God's creation," which in some translations reads "the beginning" of God's creation. Why the big difference? Why do the translators not agree? Because the underlying Greek word is the ambiguous *"arche"* (pronounced roughly as *arkay*). Jesus is the *"arche"* of God's creation. *Arche* can mean "old" or "beginning," (first) as in *"archaeology."* What is archaeology? A word brought in from the Greek meaning the study ("logos") of old things *("archae"),* that is, the study of beginnings. So the word *"arche"* can mean "beginnings." But, it can also mean ruler—the first in the kingdom and the source of power and authority. Our English word, "patri*arch,"* means "rule by the father" and "mon*archy,"* means "rule of one." Thus the word *"arche"* has a double meaning, resulting in two different ways of translating it.

If you had a Greek Old Testament and you went back to Genesis 1, you would find a very interesting thing. *"Arche"* is the first major word in the Bible—*"in the beginning God created" ("en arche").* So Revelation 3:14 contains an allusion to Genesis 1:1, pointing us to that verse. Why does John call Jesus the beginning—or the ruler—of God's creation? Apparently Jesus and Creation are a very important combination of concepts for the author of Revelation. But the association is not unique to Revelation—it is common throughout the New Testament. For example, not only does Genesis 1:1 (in Greek) start with *"en arche,"* John 1:1 begins with exactly the same—*"en arche." "In the beginning* was the Word, and the Word was with God, and the Word was God" (John 1:1, NIV).

The New Creation

Here John, the Gospel writer, is making a most interesting point: Genesis 1:1 says "in the beginning God" but John 1:1 declares that "in the beginning was the Word" (in the beginning there was Jesus). That Word that was the God of creation became flesh and lived among us. And here we find the driving force behind the Gospel of John: it is the incredible recognition that a human being who lived on earth 33 and a half years, who ministered to others, performed miracles, died and rose again, was the same One who formed the earth, said "Let there be light," created life, and made Adam out of the dust of the ground.

We find an even more fascinating reference showing that the theme of "Jesus and creation" appears widely in the New Testament: "The angel answered, 'The Holy Spirit will come upon you, and the power of the Most High will overshadow you. So the holy one to be born will be called the Son of God'" (Luke 1:35). The language here is reminiscent of Genesis 1:2: "Now the earth was formless and empty, darkness was over the surface of the deep, and the Spirit of God was hovering over the waters" (NIV). Just as the Spirit hovered over the waters of creation, now (Luke 1:35) the Spirit overshadows Mary. The Spirit was the active agent in the original creation. When the Spirit overshadowed Mary it produced a new creation—the conception of Jesus. He was conceived in Mary's womb by the action of the Holy Spirit. The earth is the old creation of the Spirit, but Jesus is the new creation.

It should not surprise us, therefore, that the New Testament also calls Jesus the new or "second" Adam (Rom. 5, 1 Cor. 15). He is the counterpart of the old Adam as much as He is the counterpart of the original creation. As such, Scripture can refer to Jesus as "the image of God" (2 Cor. 4:4, Col. 1:15, Heb. 1:3). Adam was the image of God in the original creation. But in the new creation Jesus takes the place of Adam. He becomes Adam as Adam was intended to be.

Adam as Adam Was Meant to Be

In New Testament thought this concept goes very deep. Let's take a look at the "image of God" passage in the account of creation:

"Then *God said, 'Let us make man in our image,* in our likeness, and let them rule over the fish of the sea and the birds of the air, over the livestock, over all the earth, and over all the creatures that move along the ground.'

"So God created man in his own image, in the image of God he created him; *male and female he created them.*

"God blessed them and said to them, 'Be fruitful and increase in number; fill the earth and subdue it. *Rule over the fish of the sea and the birds of the air and over every living creature that moves on the ground'* " (Gen. 1:26-28).

In the story of Genesis 1 "the image of God" manifested itself in three basic relationships, highlighted in the text above. 1. First of all, Adam was in relationship with God. As the "image of God" he had great dignity but was clearly in an inferior position to God. He was dependent on the Lord as his mentor or teacher. God was the Creator and Adam was the creature. His relationship with God was that of a subordinate to a superior.

2. The image of God included both male and female. The Creator designed Adam and Eve for relationship with each other. God did not bring Adam into existence to be alone. He created the human race for relationship among equals, regardless of gender or ethnic background (all ethnic groups share the image of God and ancestry from Adam). Ellen White addresses the former in *Patriarchs and Prophets:*

"Eve was created from a rib taken from the side of Adam, signifying that she was not to control him as the head, nor to be trampled under his feet as an inferior, but to stand by his side as an equal, to be loved and protected by him. A part of man, bone of his bone, and flesh of his flesh, she

was his second self, showing the close union and the affectionate attach-
ment that should exist in this relation" (p. 46).

3. The image of God also included dominion over the earth. Adam
ruled over the fish of the sea, the birds of the air, and the creatures that
move along the ground. Adam and Eve were to be like mentors to the animals, the plants, and the whole environment. We can illustrate the three
relationships as follows.

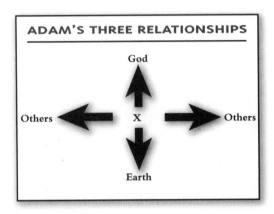

The New Testament describes Jesus as the Second Adam. He was
Adam as Adam was meant to be. Scripture describes Jesus' life on earth in
terms of Adams' experience. Do you remember the basic principle: *"God
meets people where they are"?* This holds true for the Second Adam concept
in the New Testament. As the Gospels depict Jesus' life, they do so in the
language of the original Adam and his experience.

1. *Relationship with God.* After the Fall all of Adam's relationships were
broken ones. The first to shatter was his connection with God (Gen. 3:1-
12). But Jesus came to restore Adam's broken relationships. Jesus arrived to
be Adam as Adam was meant to be. So Jesus had a perfect relationship with
God. For example He said, "the Father is greater than I" (John 14:28).
Some believe the text indicates that Jesus was inferior to God by nature.
But that is a misunderstanding. He is not inferior to God in His divine na-
ture, but as the Second Adam He took a position of subordination to the
Father. Jesus subordinated Himself to the wishes and commands of His
Father throughout His time on earth. He was demonstrating the relation-

ship that the Creator intended Adam to have. It was as the Second Adam that Jesus said such things as "I do nothing on my own but speak just what the Father has taught me" (John 8:28, NIV), and "I have obeyed my Father's commands and remain in his love" (John 15:10, NIV).

2. *Relationship with others.* Adam wasted no time putting the blame on his wife as soon as sin entered (Gen. 3:12). In contrast, Jesus had a perfect relationship with others. His whole attitude to others was one of service. In acts of loving service He illustrates a perfect relationship among human beings. He carried His willingness to serve all the way to death. Two verses state this with clarity:

"For even the Son of Man did not come to be served, but to serve, and to give his life as a ransom for many" (Mark 10:45, NIV).

"Who being in very nature God, did not consider equality with God something to be grasped, but made himself nothing, taking the very nature of a servant, being made in human likeness" (Phil. 2:6, 7).

In serving other people, Jesus demonstrated what a perfect relationship among human beings would be like. If everyone exhibited the same desire to serve and benefit others, we wouldn't have strife, war, or most of today's other problems. During His life on earth He had the kind of relationship with other people that God desired for Adam to have in the original creation.

The foot-washing service beautifully illustrates the ideal "other relationship." Jesus knew who He was. He recognized that He had come down from heaven where He had been a member of the Godhead from eternity (John 13:3). Nevertheless, He willingly performed the role of a slave (Phil. 2:6-8). He stooped down to wash His disciples' feet. It is that sort of attitude that brings peace and harmony into a relationship with others. No wonder Paul said, "Your attitude should be the same as that of Christ Jesus" (Phil. 2:5, NIV).

3. *Relationship with the earth.* In addition to a perfect relationship with God and with others, Jesus also had a perfect relationship with the environment. Again He was Adam as God had intended him to be. Like Adam, He had dominion over the fish of the sea, the birds of the air, the wind and the waves, a fact delightfully illustrated in a number of New Testament stories.

For example, one day Jesus was out in a wooden sailboat with His disciples. But a storm swept across the Sea of Galilee. Jesus was asleep in the back while the waves lashed the craft and the rain poured down. The disciples feared that the boat was going down so they roused Jesus and asked Him to intercede for them. He stood up in the boat, put up His hands, and said, "Peace, be still." The wind and the waves immediately obeyed Jesus (Matt. 8:26, 27). He had "dominion over the earth"—He was Adam as Adam was intended to be.

The original Adam's dominion included dominion over the fish of the sea (Gen. 1:26, 28). One of my favorite stories in the gospels tells of how the disciples went out fishing one night without Jesus (John 21:2-11). Why did they go out in the dark instead of during the day, when it would be more pleasant? Fishing takes place in two main ways: net fishing and lure fishing. Lure fishing requires light to attract the fish to some object that looks tasty or interesting. When the fish bites at the object, it gets caught by the hook. So lure fishing works best in the day time.

With net fishing, on the other hand, one's task is to surprise fish and catch them unawares, if possible. That's why net fishing works best at night. In the dark the fish won't always see the net coming. The creature will just be swimming along happily and suddenly it finds itself trapped. Before the fish knows what has happened, it is in the net. The disciples were doing net fishing; therefore, they fished at night. The whole night they had cast nets out into the lake, but they caught nothing. Morning came, and the sun was beginning to rise over the Galilean hills. They had one last chance to surprise some fish. If they cast the net into the shadow of the boat, fish swimming in the bright sunshine might wander into the shadow of the boat and get caught before they realized a net was there.

All of a sudden a Man stood on the beach, not far away. This Man knew a lot about preaching, but He seemed to know very little about fishing. He called out to the disciples, "Cast your net on the other side of the boat." That would have been the sunny side.

The disciples must have thought He was crazy, but they did it anyway. What happened? Fish came into that net from all over the lake. Big ones. Lots of them. Jesus didn't have to know the art of fishing, at least in human terms. He had dominion over the fish and could tell them what He wanted them to do. I can imagine Him communicating with the Galilean fish, "Hey, you, and you and you. Yes, you too! Let's go! Everybody! Into that net!" And 153 huge fish filled the disciples' nets. Why? Because Jesus was Adam as Adam was intended to be.

On another occasion Peter was talking about the need to pay some taxes (little has changed in the past 2,000 years). Jesus not only directed a fish to catch the appropriate coins; He also sent it to grab onto Peter's hook so he could retrieve the coins (Matt. 17:24-27). Christ had dominion over the fish of the sea (Gen. 1:26, 28). More than that, He had dominion over every living thing. Jesus was Adam as Adam was intended to be.

Do you remember Jesus' last ride into Jerusalem? When He rode over the Mount of Olives on an unbroken colt (Mark 11:1-7)? Have you ever tried that? I can assure you of one thing—if you try to ride an unbroken colt, it will be a very short experience and probably more exciting than any of the rides at Disneyland! It's a scary thing to mount an unbroken colt unless your name is Jesus. When Jesus sat on that colt, however, it obeyed Him like a trained animal. It recognized its Master even though it had never met Jesus before. The following box illustrates the three relationships of the Second Adam, along with sample texts.

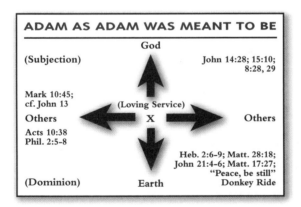

As the Second Adam, Jesus' experience was modeled on that of the first Adam. Like the first Adam, Jesus was put to sleep and an opening made in His side (Gen. 2:21-22; John 19:31-37). Out of that opening came the substances with which God created the church—blood and water (1 John 5:6). First Corinthians 11:2, 3 and Ephesians 5 describe Him as a Second Adam and the church is a second Eve—the bride of Jesus Christ.

Just as Adam and Even were together in the Garden of Eden, Jesus becomes the "husband" of His church. So New Testament writers see Adam in all of Jesus' life and experience: Adam as God created him and Adam as he was intended to be.

But not only did Jesus act out the commission of the unfallen Adam, He also succeeded where the first man failed. He was tempted along the same lines as Adam, beginning with appetite. But He did not yield to any of Satan's enticements. Jesus walked the ground where Adam had and conquered Satan at exactly the same points where the first human being failed. Jesus relived Adam's experience and redeemed Adam's failure.

A New History

This is one of the most powerful messages of salvation in the New Testament. As the Second Adam Jesus walked over the ground we all experience. Like Adam, we have a history of failure, dysfunction, and disgrace. But the story of the Second Adam tells me that Jesus has traversed the road that I have failed to complete. He has redeemed my history and made it possible for me to succeed where my ancestor Adam failed. His perfect history replaces my flawed personal history. That leaves me the hope that I can be more like the Second Adam and less like the first.

But there is more. Jesus not only redeemed Adam's failure He also reaped the consequences of that failure. When Adam sinned, he suffered its consequences—in his case thorns, sweat, nakedness, and death. Jesus, the Second Adam, also experienced all of them. He wore a crown of thorns (Gen. 3:18; Matt. 27:29), He sweat great drops of blood in Gethsemane (Gen. 3:19; Luke 22:44), and He hung naked on the cross (Gen. 3:10, 11; John 19:23, 24). And the final result of the cross, of course, was death (Gen. 2:17; 5:5; John 19:30-34).

So the Second Adam not only redeemed Adam's history (and thereby ours) but accepted its consequences so that, in Christ, we can walk in newness of life (Rom. 6:3-6). The New Testament as a whole ties the fullness of Jesus' experience to Adam. Revelation does not need to repeat all of the above. When the book of Revelation speaks of Jesus as the beginning of God's creation, it alludes to a whole sequence of ideas that first-century Christians would have readily recognized. Thus when Jesus offers Himself as the "ruler of God's creation" to the church at Laodicea (Rev. 3:14) it brings the whole Second Adam background into play. As the Second Adam He is well able to redeem His church from the lukewarmness of Laodicea.

If we didn't understand how the book of Revelation brings the whole Bible into focus, we would miss a great deal. In Revelation everything finds meaning in the light of Christ and how He fulfills the entire experience of God's Old Testament people. Whenever the New Testament writers present the Gospel, they describe it in the language, experience, and history of the Old Testament. As we gain a better understanding of this principle, Revelation becomes a new book. We can begin to experience the revelation of Jesus Christ at a deeper level than we ever imagined. In the book of Revelation "all the books of the Bible meet and end" (*The Acts of the Apostles,* p. 585).

The New Israel

In the New Testament Jesus is much more than just the Second Adam. New Testament writers described Him as a new Isaac, a new Moses, a new Joshua, a new David, a new Israel, a new Solomon, a new Elisha, and even a new Cyrus. They saw in Him a complete fulfillment of the whole Old Testament. While we don't have space to detail all of that here (you can find it in my book *Meeting God Again*), we should consider one more aspect that is extremely crucial for understanding Revelation. Jesus is the end-time fulfillment of Israel, and through Him the things of Old Testament Israel can also be applied to the church. This is addressed in one of the most important passages in Revelation:

"And they sang a new song: 'You are worthy to take the scroll and to open its seals, because you were slain, and with your blood, you purchased men for God from every tribe and language and people and nation.

" *'You have made them to be a kingdom and priests* to serve our God, and they will reign on the earth'" (Rev. 5:9, 10, NIV).

Much of the language in this text is drawn from the Old Testament. You will no doubt recognize in "they will reign on the earth" another allusion to Adam's dominion over the earth. But that is not my reason for quoting this passage here. The sentence "you have made them to be a kingdom and priests" recalls God's original charge to Israel at Mount Sinai in Exodus 19:

" 'Now if you obey me fully and keep my covenant, then out of all nations you will be my treasured possession. Although the whole earth is mine, *you will be for me a kingdom of priests* and a holy nation.' These are the words you are to speak to the Israelites" (Ex. 19:5, 6).

In Exodus 19 God founded Israel as a nation to be a kingdom of priests. It was His intention that Israel, as a people, would represent Him before the whole world. As priests they would be mediators between God and the nations, helping the other nations to understand and know God. Revelation 5 takes up the language of Israel's commissioning as a nation again—but this time applies it to the experience of God's New Testament people, those that the slain Lamb purchased with His blood from every tribe, language, people, and nation.

Thus in the New Testament Jesus is not just the Second Adam, He is also the New Israel. New Testament writers relate the experiences of Israel as a nation, from Exodus to Exile, to Jesus. Jesus goes through what Israel did and in the process succeeds where it failed, yet reaps the consequences of Israel's failure. The concept is not difficult to illustrate as it appears throughout the New Testament.

"Two men, Moses and Elijah, appeared in glorious splendor, talking with Jesus. They spoke about his *departure,* which he was about to bring to fulfillment at Jerusalem" (Luke 9:30, 31).

Luke here describes the scene of Jesus' transfiguration. Moses and Elijah speak to Him about His departure. The original Greek word is *exodos*. So they were speaking to Jesus about His *"exodus"* in Jerusalem. That "exodus" is a clear reference to the cross. Just as Israel went down to "death" at the bottom of the Red Sea and came out to a new life on the eastern shore, Jesus' death became a new Exodus for a new Israel (Matt. 2:13-15: He also becomes a new Moses for the new Israel—Acts 3:22-24 (cf. Deut. 18:15).

The New Testament writers apply the imagery of Moses, the Exodus, and Israel to the experience of Jesus in many interesting ways. Let me share a few. At Jesus' birth a hostile king wanted to take His life. In the process of trying to kill Jesus he slew all the babies in Bethlehem (Matt. 2:13-18). Do you remember that when Moses was born a hostile king also sought to destroy all the infants of Israel? He succeeded in slaying all the babies except Moses who escaped into Pharaoh's own household (Ex. 1:15-22; 2:1-10). So the experience of Jesus and Moses parallel each other.

In Exodus 33:20-23 Moses is the only Old Testament person to ever see God. The Fourth Gospel recalls this fact when it compares Moses and Jesus in John 1:17, 18. Moses fasted for 40 days on a mountaintop and then delivered the law (Ex. 24:18; 34:28). Jesus fasted for 40 days in the wilderness (Matt. 4:1-11; tradition even has it as a mountain in the wilderness of Judea) and then went up on a mountain to deliver His law—the Sermon on the Mount (Matt. 5–7). Furthermore, Moses appointed 70 elders (Num. 11:16-30) and Jesus had 70 disciples (Luke 10:1). God glorified Moses on a mountain (Ex. 34:29-35) and at the time of His transfiguration, He did the same for Jesus (Matt. 17:1-8). We could cite many other parallels between Moses and Jesus, but the ones mentioned here are enough to give the flavor. The New Testament writers understood Jesus to be a new Moses—a new lawgiver and a new teacher of a new Israel.

The book of Matthew also sees Jesus as a new Israel, for example. Matthew tells us that Jesus had to go down to Egypt and return because Israel was called to its destiny out of Egypt (Matt. 2:13-15; Hosea 11:1-9). After He is brought up from Egypt, He passes through the water of baptism (Matt. 3; Luke 3) just as Israel did through the waters of the Red Sea (Ex. 14, 15). Then Jesus spends 40 days in the wilderness (Matt. 4:1-11; Luke 4:1-13) just as Israel, after going through the Red Sea, lived 40 years in the wilderness (Num. 14:33, 34). While we don't have time to note every parallel, the examples I have cited illustrate how the New Testament writers saw Jesus' life, death, and resurrection as a replay of the experiences of Moses and Israel.

Do you remember a principle we discussed earlier in this book? *Since God meets people where they are, He uses the language of the past to describe His actions in the present and the future.* If you want to understand what God seeks to accomplish through His Word, you must first recognize how that language spoke to that time and place—it is the vocabulary of that prophet's past. That's why the language of the New Testament sounds so much like that of the Old Testament—God was meeting them where they were.

Jesus is the new Israel in the New Testament. Not only does He relive the experience of the old Israel, He obeys God in the very circumstances in which Israel failed. He also suffered the consequences of Israel's failure, just as He did the results of Adam's sin. Thus Jesus experienced the curses of Israel's breaking of the covenant. A quick reading of

Deuteronomy 28 is sufficient to show the many ways in which Jesus' experience paralleled the results of Israel's disobedience.

Deuteronomy 28 predicted that a rebellious Israel would be stripped of its wealth and force to live in poverty (Deut. 28:15-20). Matthew 8:20 tells us that Jesus had nowhere to lay His head. The cursed ones of Deuteronomy 28 were to be "smitten before your enemies" (verse 25), and this certainly took place on the cross. Among the other curses of Deuteronomy 28 was darkness (Matt. 27:45), being mocked (Mark 15:20, 31), hunger (Matt. 4:2), thirst (John 19:28), and nakedness (Matt. 27:35). With the possible exception of hunger, all of these had a fulfillment in Jesus' ordeal at the cross.

The climax of the curses in Deuteronomy 28 appears in verses 65-67. Israel would be cursed with an anxious mind and a despairing heart. Jesus experienced the same at a place called Gethsemane (Mark 14:32-42). So we see powerful connections also between the curses of the covenant and what Jesus went through. He not only relives the history of Israel and redeems it, He also takes up the curses of Israel and experiences them. Jesus is the complete historical counterpart of Israel, redeeming its failures and exhausting the curses of the covenant against the nation.

All this is important when it comes to understanding Revelation 5:9, 10. When the passage applies the language of Old Testament Israel to the church, it is understandable because Jesus Christ is the new Israel. Who was the old Israel? The first Israel was Jacob, who received the spiritual name Israel when he entered into a covenant with God (Gen. 32:24-30). Jacob had 12 sons. Their descendants became the 12 tribes of Israel. So the original Israel started out as a family. Jesus, as the new Israel, also developed a family—the 12 disciples. No doubt He selected exactly 12 disciples because He knew that His experience was to be modeled on Old Testament Israel.

Israel, Jesus, and the Church

Just as Christ fulfilled the history of Israel in His own life, therefore, the experience of the church is also modeled on that history. So when the New Testament talks about the church it often does so in the language of Israel. That means, for example, that when Revelation introduces the 144,000, 12,000 from each of the 12 tribes of Israel, it is probably talking about the church as 12 spiritual tribes descended from the witness of the 12 apostles (Matt. 19:27, 28). The church, in the book of Revelation and throughout the New Testament, is patterned after the experience of Old Testament Israel.

So the church really has two models for its behavior. On the one hand, it echoes Old Testament Israel. In the book of Revelation the church battles with Sodom, Egypt, and Babylon just as Old Testament Israel did. John describes the history of the church in the vocabulary of the past, the language of the Old Testament. But we have already seen that Jesus went through all the experiences of Old Testament Israel. So the church also models on Jesus Christ. "Where I am, there also will my servant be" (John 12:26).

Thus Jesus' life, death, and resurrection become models for the life,

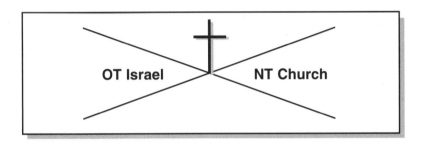

experience, and behavior of the church. The book of Revelation illustrates it in some fascinating ways—the church is pursued into the wilderness (Rev. 12:6, 14), is put to death (Rev. 6:9, 10), endures suffering (Rev. 13:9, 10; 12:14), is made up of kings and priests (Rev. 1:5, 6; 5:9, 10), serves 1260 days clothed in sackcloth (Rev. 11:3—Jesus' ministry was 3½ years long), is slain and mocked (Rev. 11:7-10), but is also resurrected and ascends to heaven (Rev. 11:11, 12). So the book of Revelation describes the church in terms of both Jesus and Israel. But in what sense can we call the church Israel? Is it ethnic, geographic, or relational?

The Ethnic Option. In ethnic terms, Israel started out as a birth family with 12 sons physically descended from Jacob. They became a race and then a nation. Can we refer to the church as Israel in an ethnic sense? No. Revelation 5:9, 10 tells us that on the cross Jesus purchased His followers from every tribe, people, language, and nation and made them to be a kingdom of priests. So Revelation applies the language of Israel to all the people of the earth who accept Jesus Christ. Whoever is in relationship with Him belongs to Israel because Jesus is the new Israel. The language of Revelation 7 sounds as if the 144,000 are exclusively of the ethnic tribes of Israel, but the things of Israel have been expanded through Christ.

Jesus, the new Israel, has relived the history of ancient Israel. Anyone who is in relationship with Jesus, therefore, is adopted into the family of the new Jacob. It doesn't matter if you are German, African, Australian, Indian, or Chinese—it does not matter where you are from or what your ethnic background is—if you are in relationship with Jesus Christ, then you are part of the family of Israel. So when Revelation speaks of the attributes of Israel, we should not think in ethnic terms. It is no longer whom you are descended from but whom you are related to that counts.

The Geographical Option. Old Testament Israel was geographically oriented. The family/nation became attached to a particular place. They had borders—borders that would change from time to time—but were reasonably identifiable. Whenever individual Israelites moved away from that national territory, they would seize every opportunity to travel back home, particularly to Jerusalem. Should we think of the church as Israel in geographical terms? The answer is also no. Jesus, the new Israel, is located in heavenly places (Rev. 5:6-14; 7:15-17). No place on earth is closer to Him than any other. Thus no matter where you live you have equal access to Him through the Holy Spirit.

To refer to the church in terms of Israel, then, is speak of it in relationship to Jesus Christ. So while Revelation uses Old Testament language about Israel and its neighbors, its significance is neither ethnic nor geographical. We must not understand Babylon, the Euphrates River, Jezebel, David, Egypt, and Sodom in the old ethnic or geographical sense. Instead, they have to do with Jesus, the church, and the challenges the church faces in the course of Christian history.

Spiritual and Worldwide

The book of Revelation uses the language of the Old Testament but the meaning is different. John applies physical things involving Israel and its neighbors in a spiritual and worldwide sense. The new Israel is not located in any one specific place or made up of any one particular people. Anyone in any place who is related to Jesus Christ can become a part of that new Israel.

If that is true, it has powerful implications for the interpretation of Revelation. Anyone who misses this point will have as much difficulty understanding the book as will those who have never heard of the Old Testament. So we must be honest and say that many sincere Christians do not read Revelation in the right way. They believe that Revelation is not written to Christians but to ethnic Jews living at the end of time. Thus it really has nothing to do with the church, even though both the beginning (Rev. 1:11, 19) and the end (Rev. 22:16) seem to say that it does.

While I respect all godly Christians who differ, I think the point is not hard to demonstrate, beginning with Revelation 5:9, 10. There John takes the language of God's Old Testament people, an ethnic group heading for a geographical place, and applies it to those purchased by the cross, to people from every tribe, language, and nation. The Israel of Revelation has no ethnic or geographical limitation.

Revelation 7:4-8 describes a group of 144,000 individuals made up of 12,000 from each of the 12 tribes of Israel. But John never sees this group. Instead, he looks and sees a great multitude beyond numbering, made up of people from every tribe, language, and nation (verses 9, 10). So when he hears about 144,000 Israelites he is not thinking ethnically about Israel. Israel has spiritual, worldwide characteristics in his book.

But let's put this thesis to the test by examining a specific geographical term in Revelation 16:12: "The sixth angel poured out his bowl on the great river Euphrates, and its water was dried up to prepare the way for the kings from the East" (NIV). If you want to take the language of Revelation literally, the Euphrates River must mean an actual geographical spot in the Middle East (in modern day Iraq). But is that what the book of Revelation has in mind? If you had to decide between an answer someone gave you and one the author himself provides, which would you choose? Obviously, the author of a book should have the privilege of telling us what he means by any symbol he uses. And that's exactly what John does in this case. Let's explore this question by looking at Revelation 17:1.

"One of the seven angels *who had the seven bowls* came and said to me, 'Come, I will show you the punishment of the great prostitute, who sits on *many waters*'" (NIV). I want you to notice two things in this text. First, one of the bowl angels of chapter 16 has come to explain something, and, second, that it has to do with "many waters." So which of the seven bowl angels is this? Which of the seven bowls have anything to do with water? That would be the second (Rev. 16:3—falls on the sea), the third (verses 4-7—rivers and springs), and the sixth (verse 12—Euphrates River). Thus the angels would be either the second, third, or sixth. But let's be more specific.

"This title was written on her forehead: MYSTERY, BABYLON THE GREAT, THE MOTHER OF PROSTITUTES AND OF THE ABOMINATIONS OF THE EARTH" (Rev. 17:5, NIV). What is Babylon? It was an ancient city located on the Euphrates River. So when you talk about a woman who sits on many waters (verse 1) and whose name is Babylon (verse 5), there is no question exactly what the waters of Revelation 17:1 are—the Euphrates River (see "many waters" in Jer. 51:13). The angel who approaches John in Revelation 17 is the sixth bowl angel. He has come to tell something about the Euphrates River, an explanation that appears in Revelation 17:15.

"Then the angel said to me, 'The waters you saw, where the prostitute sits, *are peoples, multitudes, nations and languages'*" (NIV). What are the "waters you saw?" They are the waters of verse 1, the waters of the Euphrates River. What does the Euphrates River represent? In verse 15 the angel tells us exactly: "peoples, multitudes, nations and languages." The Euphrates River is a symbol of many nations—the political, secular, and economic powers of our world. In the Old Testament the Euphrates River was a literal and local body of water, but in the book of Revelation it is a symbol of a worldwide spiritual concept.

The principle of "spiritual and worldwide" is not difficult to demonstrate throughout the book of Revelation. In Zechariah 12:10 the "inhabitants of Jerusalem" mourn over the one they have pierced. Then in Revelation 1:7 "every eye" will mourn in the language of Zechariah. What the Jerusalemites do in Zechariah the whole world does in Revelation. Isaiah 34:9, 10 describes the land of Edom (a small nation in the Old Testament) as burning forever, its smoke ascending, while in Revelation 14:10, 11 this is the experience of everyone in the world who receives the mark of the beast. Joel 3:12, 13 sets the tiny "Valley of Jehoshaphat" outside Jerusalem as the scene of the final battle between Judah and its enemies, while in Revelation 14:14-20 "outside the city" clearly has to do with the whole world.

So the book of Revelation treats Israel, its neighbors, and even

Babylon and its river in a spiritual, worldwide sense. The key to the language is relationship with Jesus Christ. Those who are on the side of the Lamb are ranked with Israel. But those who find themselves in opposition to God are Babylon, Egypt, Edom, and the Euphrates River. Just as we must understand Israel as spiritual and worldwide, so Babylon in Revelation is also spiritual and worldwide.

Spiritual and Worldwide in Revelation	
Literal and Local (OT)	Spiritual and Worldwide (Rev.)
Euphrates River	Peoples, nations, languages (Rev. 17:15)
Inhabitants of Jerusalem (Zech. 12:10)	"Every eye" (Rev. 1:7)
Edom (Isa. 34:8–10)	All who have the Mark of the Beast (Rev. 14:9, 10)
Israel at Sinai (Ex. 19:5, 6)	Some from every tribe, language and nation (Rev, 1:5, 6; 5:9, 10)
Valley of Jehoshaphat (Joel 3)	Earth (Rev. 14:14–20)

This principle is crucial for interpreting Revelation. If you read into it the literal and local things of the Old Testament, you will misunderstand the whole purpose and intent of the book. You will have a great deal of difficulty finding Jesus Christ in Revelation, and Jesus Christ is what the whole book is supposed to be about. The book of Revelation is not "The Revelation of the Middle East," nor is it "The Revelation of Modern-day Israel." Rather, it is "The Revelation of Jesus Christ" (Rev. 1:1) and of His church (Rev. 22:16)—about Jesus and the people who are in relationship to Him (Rev. 17:14).

If a method of interpretation does not bring Jesus into clearer focus, it is not helping us to understand the book of Revelation. In the book of Revelation all the other books of the Bible meet and end. It makes the Old Testament come alive because it baptizes the things of the Old Testament into Jesus Christ and applies them to people who are living in the last days. So the book of Revelation can make the Old Testament relevant for God's people today.

Finding Christ in the Trumpet Plagues

But I sense that you still have doubts. For example, how can the plagues of the book be a revelation of Jesus Christ? How can the horrible events of the seals and the trumpets shed any light on the gospel? *Perhaps you can find Christ in other parts of the book,* you may be thinking, *but what about all the horror stuff?*

OK, let's take up the challenge. To conclude this book on method let's go to the most horrible, most perplexing, most difficult passage in the book: the fifth trumpet (Rev. 9:1-11). If you can find Jesus there, you can find Him anywhere.

"The fifth angel sounded his trumpet, and I saw a star that had fallen from the sky to the earth. The star was given the key to the shaft of the Abyss. When he opened the Abyss, smoke rose from it like the smoke from a gigantic furnace. The sun and sky were darkened by the smoke from the Abyss. And out of the smoke locusts came down upon the earth and were given power like that of scorpions of the earth. They were told not to harm the grass of the earth or any plant or tree, but only those people who did not have the seal of God on their foreheads. They were not given power to kill them, but only to torture them for five months. And the agony they suffered was like that of the sting of a scorpion when it strikes a man. During those days men will seek death, but will not find it; they will long to die, but death will elude them" (Rev. 9:1-6, NIV).

At first glance, is this a typical presentation of the gospel? Does Jesus seem visible anywhere? Or is this passage more like a horror show? I once made the mistake of trying to dramatize this passage for a children's story in church (my wife doesn't always vouch for my sanity)! I told the kids about the trumpet and the falling star and the Abyss (or bottomless pit). After describing the darkness, I then portrayed giant locusts flying around with huge stingers that would sneak up behind people and stab them in the seat cushions! Before I could finish I noticed a couple of girls around 12 years of age looking horribly frightened. I made a mental note to apologize to them and their parents after church. When the service finished, I asked for them and learned that they had become ill and had to go home early. And I never saw them again! Not much gospel on the surface of this text! Handle with care.

So where is Jesus Christ in the plagues of the fifth trumpet? Where is

Jesus in the Abyss or the darkness? And where is Jesus in the stings of the locust/scorpions? If you can find Him in this passage, He must be everywhere in the book! Let's follow the method outlined previously and see what we learn. We will compare this passage in the trumpets with parallel texts in the New Testament and see if they clarify the gospel meaning of these images.

First of all, the passage mentions an Abyss. In verse 1 a fallen star receives a key from heaven to open up the shaft leading into the Abyss. From Luke 8:30-32 we gain some insight into the Abyss. It is the passage about Jesus' encounter with a demoniac and the demons within him: "Jesus asked him, 'What is your name?' 'Legion,' he replied, because many demons had gone into him. And they begged him repeatedly not to order them to go into the Abyss" (NIV). Whatever we understand by "Abyss" it is clearly a place where demons do not want to go, where they are confined and prevented from the kinds of activity that they prefer. So opening the Abyss would prepare the way for a demonic attack on the inhabitants of the earth. But the key to the Abyss comes down out of heaven, suggesting that such a demonic attack somehow serves God's purpose.

In the second verse the focus of the plague is on darkness. Smoke rises out of the Abyss like the fumes of a great furnace (Sodom—Gen. 19). And the smoke from the Abyss darkens the air and sky. The New Testament has a consistent theme of light and darkness. Jesus is the light of the world (John 8:12; 9:5). Wherever He goes light floods into the world (John 3:18-21). How people respond to that light determines their relationship with Jesus and their ultimate destiny. Darkness, on the other hand, spells the absence of Jesus and the gospel. So in the fifth trumpet this demonic plague blots out the view of Jesus and the knowledge of the gospel from the world. Whatever the fifth trumpet is about, it results in a lack of Jesus' presence and the truth about Him.

Is there any good news in this passage? Yes, there is. In Revelation 9:3, 4 the smoke resolves itself into locusts with scorpion stingers. While it might seem like further horror, it actually brings the first sign of good news. The locust/scorpions are given a restriction, a limitation, being told "not to harm the grass of the earth or any plant or tree, but *only those people who did not have the seal of God on their foreheads*" (NIV). These are strange locusts! Normally locusts feed on vegetation and leave people

173

alone. These locusts symbolize God's judgments on human beings. But those judgments involve only those not on God's side. So this demonic plague cannot hurt those whom God has sealed.

One text in the New Testament takes up more of this language than any other, and that is Luke 10:17-20. I italicize the language that reflects Greek words and themes also found in the fifth trumpet:

"The seventy-two returned with joy and said, 'Lord, even the demons submit to us in your name.' He replied, 'I saw Satan *fall like lightning from heaven.* I have given you *authority to trample on snakes and scorpions* and to overcome all *the power of the enemy; nothing will *harm* you. However, do not rejoice that *the spirits* submit to you, but rejoice that your names are written in heaven'" (Luke 10:17-20, NIV).

The two texts have seven or eight major words in common between them. While we cannot be certain that John ever saw a copy of Luke, he must have been familiar with this saying of Christ. The disciples of Jesus received His power over the demons, and their names were written in heaven. And from that assurance they discovered that all the power of the enemy could not harm them. To those who are in relationship with Jesus the demonic "sting of the scorpion" has no power to hurt. Luke 10 confirms that scorpions are a symbol of satanic power on earth.

The passage also helps us see Jesus in Revelation 9. At some point in history (leaving the details for another book) God permits an unlocking of the Abyss. The result of that action is massive demonic attack against our world. It will strike at people's knowledge of God and seek to obliterate the good news of the gospel from the earth. When that assault comes Jesus will be a shelter and a comfort to His people. The demonic attack will have no power over them. Satan will be able to hurt only those who have allowed him control over their lives. The lion can roar. He can rattle the windows and try to block up people's way in life. But his power to hurt and to kill is subject to the authority of Jesus. The disciple need not be afraid.

The message of the fifth trumpet turns out to be roughly the same as that of Romans 8:35-39:

"Who shall separate us from the love of Christ? Shall trouble or hardship or persecution or famine or nakedness or danger or sword? As it is written: 'For your sake we face death all day long; we are considered as sheep to be slaughtered.' No, in all these things we are more than conquerors

through him who loved us. For I am convinced that neither death nor life, *neither angels nor demons,* neither the present nor the future, *nor any powers,* neither height nor depth, nor anything else in all creation, *will be able to separate us from the love of God that is in Christ Jesus our Lord"* (NIV).

Seeing Christ in the book of Revelation

1. Collect potential New Testament parallel texts.
   - ✔ Bible margins
   - ✔ Commentaries
   - ✔ Concordances
   - ✔ Computer Bible programs
2. Copy the passage in Revelation and the potential parallels texts in large print.
3. Using a colored pen or highlighter, mark all significant parallel words.
4. Use a concordance to seek out thematic parallels and echoes of New Testament theology.
5. Through a broad-reading approach, constantly upgrade your understanding of the main themes of the New Testament.
6. Try to determine how the gospel of Jesus Christ affects each passage of Revelation.

Conclusion

It is hard to imagine horrors greater than those portrayed in the book of Revelation. The vision piles one terrible image upon another. But the purpose of the whole book is not to entertain or to intimidate. The intent of Revelation's horrors is to highlight the grace of God in Jesus Christ. No matter how bad things get, the gospel still wins. No matter how out of control events seem, God is still in control. Our eyes and our ears tell us that things are falling apart, that there is no safety anywhere. But the book of Revelation directs our attention beyond the reality we can perceive. Revelation points us to a God who sent His Son to die for us, that we might have life—a more abundant life. And the Lamb that was slain (Rev. 5:5, 6) is alive again forevermore (Rev. 1:17, 18). Those in relationship with Him can overcome by the blood of the Lamb and the word of their testimony (Rev. 12:11, 12). And in the end evil, terrorism, hatred, war, and abuse will cease (Rev. 21:3, 4). We will see Jesus' face (Rev. 22:4). And God will wipe every tear from our eyes (Rev. 7:16, 17).